my **revisi**

Sut

D1103613

OCR
COMPUTING
for GCSE
COMPUTER SYSTEMS
AND PROGRAMMING

Title in this series:

OCR Computing for GCSE Student's Book

978-1-4441-7779-4

To order visit www.hoddereducation.co.uk

my **revisi**n notes

OCR
Official Publisher Partnership

HODDER
EDUCATION

OCR
COMPUTING
for GCSE
COMPUTER SYSTEMS
AND PROGRAMMING

Sean O'Byrne and George Rouse

HODDER
EDUCATION
AN HACHETTE UK COMPANY

The publisher would like to thank the following for permission to reproduce copyright material:

Photo credits:

3 *t* © Rainer Plendl – Fotolia; *b* © 3d brained – Fotolia; **4** © Mikhail Basov – Fotolia; **13** *t* © mrkob – Fotolia; *b l* © Stephen Hilger/Bloomberg via Getty Images; *b r* © Scanrail – Fotolia; **15** © George Rouse; **16** *t* © George Rouse; *c l* © picsfive – Fotolia; *c r* © mrkob – Fotolia; *b* © mrkob – Fotolia; **17** *t* © Photofusion Picture Library / Alamy; *c l* © AP/Press Association Images; *c r* © amorphis – Fotolia; *b* © George Rouse; **18** *t l* © dja65 – Fotolia; *t r* © Joel Saget/AFP Photo/Getty Images; *c l* © Moreno Soppelsa – Fotolia; *c r* © George Rouse; *b* © LINAK A/S; **19** *t* © Alexandr Mitiuc – Fotolia; *c* © showcake – Fotolia; *b* © Nrbelex http://upload.wikimedia.org/wikipedia/commons/2/2c/USB_flash_drive.JPG?uselang=en-gb http://creativecommons.org/licenses/by-sa/3.0/deed.en; **21** *t l* © Nikolai Sorokin – Fotolia; *t c* © Roberto – Fotolia; *t r* © amorphis – Fotolia; *b l* © kartos – Fotolia; *b r* © rnophoto – Fotolia; **25** *t* © bloomua – Fotolia; *b* © Sean O'Byrne; **40** *t l* © George Rouse ; *t r* Vasiliy Vasilyev, HHD Software Ltd; **52** *t* Libre Office; *c* Libre Office; **56** *t* © horvathta – Fotolia; *b* © Olivier Le Moal – Fotolia; **57** *t* © sheval – Fotolia; *b* © amorphis – Fotolia; **70** © Sean O'Byrne

Although every effort has been made to ensure that website addresses are correct at time of going to press, Hodder Education cannot be held responsible for the content of any website mentioned. It is sometimes possible to find a relocated web page by typing in the address of the home page for a website in the URL window of your browser.

Orders: please contact Bookpoint Ltd, 130 Milton Park, Abingdon, Oxon OX14 4SB. Telephone: (44) 01235 827720. Fax: (44) 01235 400454. Lines are open 9.00–17.00, Monday to Saturday, with a 24-hour message answering service. Visit our website at www.hoddereducation.co.uk

© Sean O'Byrne, George Rouse 2013

First published in 2013 by

Hodder Education

An Hachette UK Company,

338 Euston Road

London NW1 3BH

Impression number	5	4		
Year	2017	2016	2015	2014

Cover photo © vege – Fotolia

Typeset in CronosPro 12 pts by Datapage (India) Pvt. Ltd.

Printed and bound in Spain

A catalogue record for this title is available from the British Library

ISBN 978 1 444 193848

Get the most from this book

This book will help you revise the new OCR GCSE Computing specification. You can use the Contents list to plan your revision, topic by topic. Tick each box when you have:

1 revised and understood a topic

2 tested yourself

3 checked your answers online.

You can also keep track of your revision by ticking off each topic heading through the book. You may find it helpful to add your own notes as you work through each topic.

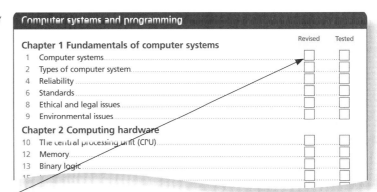

Tick to track your progress

Exam tip

Throughout the book there are Exam tips that explain how you can boost your final grade.

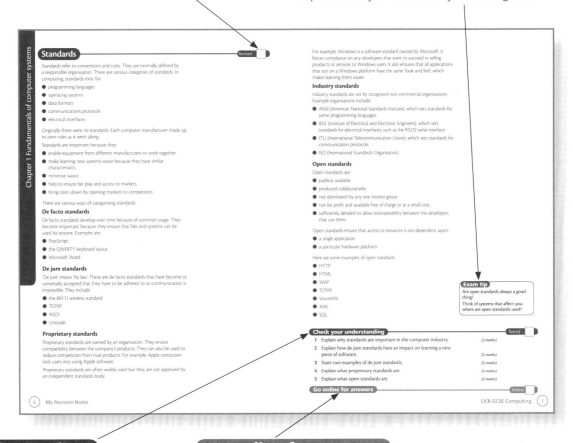

Check your understanding

Use these questions at the end of each section to make sure that you have understood every topic.

Go online for answers

Go online to check your answers at
www.therevisionbutton.co.uk/myrevisionnotes

Contents and revision planner

Computer systems and programming

Chapter 1 Fundamentals of computer systems

Computer systems

Revised

A **computer** is an electronic, programmable data processing machine.

A **system** is a collection of parts that work together for some defined purpose.

A **computer system** is a collection of hardware and software that works together to achieve some data processing task.

Systems receive **inputs** from the outside. They **process** these inputs. They **output** the results of the processing.

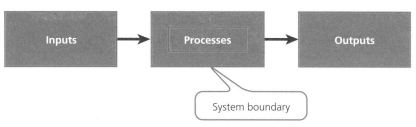

↑ **Figure 1.1 Outline of a system**

A system is separated from the outside world by a **system boundary**. These boundaries are often called **interfaces**.

Importance of computer systems

Most aspects of our lives are affected by computer systems. They have led to:

● improved quality in manufacturing – robotic machinery is more accurate than humans

● cheaper manufacturing – automation reduces wage costs and allows 24/7 working

● faster access to information – many jobs can be done more quickly

● better decision making – with lots of facts organised and available, decisions can be better informed

● new ways of doing business – more buying online, more choice, cheaper goods; facilities such as the internet and ATMs would not be possible without computer systems

● new ways of communicating – email, SMS, cell phones – are being developed all the time.

Examples of computer systems

Computer system	Inputs (examples)	Outputs (examples)	Processing
car engine management	temperature, CO_2 levels, speed	signals to carburettor, data to engine diagnostics	check values against set parameters, produce fault codes
holiday booking	dates, destinations, credit card details	itineraries, air tickets, hotel reservations	check availability, produce documents

Computer system	Inputs (examples)	Outputs (examples)	Processing
washing machine	temperature, water levels, dirtiness	signals to motor, heater, timer	check values, determine washing parameters
satnav	signals from satellites, inputs from user	route, places of interest, warnings	check position, locate on map, output map
ATM (automated teller machine) or cash point	card details, PIN, user requests	balance, cash	check balance, adjust balance of account
travel card e.g. Oyster card	location of station, bus route number, top-up information, money	open gate to station, display balance	calculate journey cost, adjust balance

Exam tip

Try to identify lots of computer systems. They are everywhere these days.

Questions may be set on unfamiliar systems. Identify inputs, processing and outputs for a wide variety of systems.

Check your understanding

Tested

For a digital camera, state:

a) two input devices   (2 marks)

b) two output devices   (2 marks)

c) one storage device.   (1 mark)

Go online for answers

Online

Types of computer system

Revised

General-purpose systems

Personal computers such as desktops, laptops, notebooks and tablet computers, as well as smart phones, are designed to perform multiple tasks. Various **applications** (apps) can be loaded so that they can be used for a wide variety of purposes.

Dedicated systems

Dedicated systems are specially produced to perform a single function or set of functions. For example, a ticket-vending machine at a train station is not likely to be used for any other purpose.

Control systems

Control systems are computer systems that control machinery, rather than produce output for humans to read or respond to. They are particularly important in manufacturing processes but are increasingly part of common domestic and personal gadgets.

Industrial robots are an important application of control systems.

↑ Figure 1.2 Industrial robots manufacturing cars

Embedded systems

Embedded systems are computer systems that are part of a larger system. They are usually also control systems. They include portable devices:

- digital watches
- satnavs
- cameras
- MP3 players.

They also include larger installations, such as:

- traffic lights
- controllers of machinery in factories.

Embedded systems can be very simple or highly complex, such as the avionics systems in aircraft. Most cars now have up to 50 computer systems looking after things like fuel flow, window control, cruise control and fault management.

Expert systems

Expert systems are computer systems designed to behave like a human expert. They have three component parts:

- a knowledge base (a database of facts)
- an inference engine (software that makes deductions using the knowledge base)
- an interface (to allow a human user access to the system).

They are commonly used for:

- diagnosing diseases
- finding faults in machinery
- choosing complex products, such as mortgages and insurance policies
- suggesting purchases to consumers
- making credit checks.

↑ Figure 1.3 GPS navigation system

Exam tip

Think of the advantages of using embedded systems in a wide variety of devices. How are device faults diagnosed and repaired?

Exam tip

Think of the advantages and disadvantages of relying on expert systems.

Management information systems

Management information systems bring together the information from all parts of an organisation so that managers can make sensible decisions. They cover:

● technology

● data

● people.

They typically produce regular reports based on the organisation's data.

Examples of management information systems:

● Decision Support Systems are used by middle management to support day-to-day decision making.

● Executive Information Systems produce reports using data from throughout an organisation and support decisions about the organisation's strategy.

● Office Automation Systems automate workflow and maximise the efficiency of data movement.

● School Management Information Systems deal with school administration, teaching and learning.

Check your understanding   Tested ☐

1 Define the term 'embedded system'.   *(2 marks)*

2 Give two uses of an expert system.   *(2 marks)*

3 State the three main component parts of an expert system.   *(3 marks)*

Go online for answers   Online ☐

Reliability   Revised ☐

Computers are central to most of our work and leisure activities. They also play a central part in many life-or-death situations:

● aircraft navigation and control

● railway signalling

● many medical situations.

Medical computer systems include activities such as:

● record keeping

● diagnosis of diseases

● CAT (computer axial tomography) scans

● drug interactions

● use of search engines and expert systems to check symptoms

● robotic or remote surgery

● DNA sequencing.

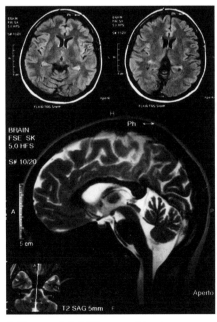

↑ **Figure 1.4 CAT scan of brain**

Reliability is expected when new computer systems are commissioned. Mistakes in the design and production of systems can lead to:

- down time
- expensive errors
- data loss
- compromised privacy.

Exam tip

Extended response questions might give prompts such as:

Be aware of ways in which privacy can be invaded by modern computer systems. How much does it matter?

Data integrity

Reliability also refers to data **integrity**. This relates to data being accurate and consistent throughout its life. Data integrity also means that the stored data reflects real-world reality. Database systems normally have rules that prevent inconsistent changes being made to the underlying data.

Data integrity can be compromised by:

- human errors when data is entered
- errors that occur when data is transmitted from one computer to another
- software bugs
- viruses and other malware
- hardware malfunctions
- natural disasters.

Ways to reduce risks to data include:

- backing up data regularly
- controlling access to data via security mechanisms
- using validation rules to prevent the input of invalid data
- using error detection and correction software when transmitting data.

Exam tip

Think of various ways of backing up and otherwise safeguarding data. How do **you** back your data up?

Reliability and testing

Reliability is improved by thorough testing. Testing is designed to uncover errors.

Testing can never be complete because:

- software is so complex
- testing is expensive
- testing is time consuming.

There are huge numbers of pathways through most modern systems so there are usually errors even in extensively tested systems.

Check your understanding ———————————————————— Tested

1 State two ways that computers are used in medicine. *(2 marks)*
2 Define the term 'data integrity'. *(2 marks)*
3 Describe two ways in which data integrity can be compromised. *(2 marks)*
4 State the purpose of software testing. *(2 marks)*
5 Explain why software often still has errors after it has been released. *(2 marks)*

Go online for answers ———————————————————— Online

Standards

Standards refer to conventions and rules. They are normally defined by a responsible organisation. There are various categories of standards. In computing, standards exist for:

- programming languages
- operating systems
- data formats
- communications protocols
- electrical interfaces.

Originally there were no standards. Each computer manufacturer made up its own rules as it went along.

Standards are important because they:

- enable equipment from different manufacturers to work together
- make learning new systems easier because they have similar characteristics
- minimise waste
- help to ensure fair play and access to markets
- bring costs down by opening markets to competition.

There are various ways of categorising standards.

De facto standards

De facto standards develop over time because of common usage. They become important because they ensure that files and systems can be used by anyone. Examples are:

- PostScript
- the QWERTY keyboard layout
- Microsoft Word.

De jure standards

'De jure' means 'by law'. These are de facto standards that have become so universally accepted that they have to be adhered to or communication is impossible. They include:

- the 801.11 wireless standard
- TCP/IP
- ASCII
- PDF
- Unicode.

Proprietary standards

Proprietary standards are owned by an organisation. They ensure compatibility between the company's products. They can also be used to reduce competition from rival products. For example, Apple computers lock users into using Apple software.

Proprietary standards are often widely used but they are not approved by an independent standards body.

For example, Windows is a software standard owned by Microsoft. It forces compliance on any developers that want to succeed in selling products or services to Windows users. It also ensures that all applications that run on a Windows platform have the same 'look and feel', which makes learning them easier.

Industry standards

Industry standards are set by recognised non-commercial organisations. Example organisations include:

- ANSI (American National Standards Institute), which sets standards for some programming languages
- IEEE (Institute of Electrical and Electronic Engineers), which sets standards for electrical interfaces, such as the RS232 serial interface
- ITU (International Telecommunication Union), which sets standards for communication protocols
- ISO (International Standards Organisation).

Open standards

Open standards are:

- publicly available
- produced collaboratively
- not dominated by any one interest group
- not for profit and available free of charge or at a small cost
- sufficiently detailed to allow interoperability between the developers that use them.

Open standards ensure that access to resources is not dependent upon:

- a single application
- a particular hardware platform.

Here are some examples of open standards:

- HTTP
- HTML
- WAP
- TCP/IP
- VoiceXML
- XML
- SQL.

> **Exam tip**
>
> Are open standards always a good thing?
>
> Think of systems that affect you: where are open standards used?

Check your understanding

Tested

1. Explain why standards are important in the computer industry. *(3 marks)*
2. Explain how de jure standards have an impact on learning a new piece of software. *(2 marks)*
3. State two examples of de jure standards. *(2 marks)*
4. Explain what proprietary standards are. *(2 marks)*
5. Explain what open standards are. *(2 marks)*

Go online for answers

Online

Ethical and legal issues

Like any other tools, computer systems can be used for good or ill. Making choices between doing good or doing harm is a matter of ethics.

Just as in any other aspect of human life, governments try (or should try) to make laws in order to protect their citizens from harm.

An **ethical** act is one that is morally 'right'.

A **legal** act is one that does not break any laws.

Widespread computer use has produced some new legal and ethical challenges. These are to do with aspects of life such as:

- privacy
- data security
- espionage
- access to sensitive data
- fair charging for services
- copyright
- terrorism.

Exam tip

Make sure you clearly understand the difference between 'ethical' and 'legal'.

Data protection

Most governments have enacted laws that are intended to protect the privacy of individuals when data about them is stored on computer systems. For example, the UK Data Protection Act covers any data about a living and identifiable individual. The reasons why such legislation is needed are because it is so easy to:

- copy data
- transmit data
- match data and make judgements about people.

Typical data protection laws include provisions that organisations must:

- allow people to view the data held about them
- correct information when requested
- not use data in any way that may potentially cause damage or distress
- allow people to state that their data is not to be used for direct marketing
- adequately protect data from unauthorised access
- only collect data for a specified and lawful purpose
- not transmit personal data outside the European Economic Area.

Other laws exist that make it illegal to access or modify unauthorised computer material.

Nowadays there are numerous examples of **cyber crime** (crimes committed with the aid of computers) but they are difficult to police because the internet crosses international boundaries and local laws differ so much.

1　Explain the difference between ethical and legal issues.　　*(2 marks)*

2　State three provisions of a typical data protection law.　　*(3 marks)*

3　Explain what is meant by cyber crime.　　*(1 mark)*

Go online for answers　　　　　　　　　　　　　Online

Environmental issues　　　　　　　　　　　Revised

Widespread computer use is in many ways good for the environment. In particular, it reduces the need for travel and the transport of goods. Manufactured goods can be made by robots to a greater degree of accuracy than by humans. This can lead to more efficient products that last longer and use energy more efficiently.

However, the abundance of computers poses its own special environmental problems.

Waste

Obsolete computers have to be disposed of. They contain toxic materials such as:

● lead

● cadmium

● beryllium

● flame retardants.

E-waste is often shipped to developing countries where there are few safeguards. Much waste goes to landfill, where toxic chemicals can leach out into the soil. Old computers contain a lot of plastics, for example, in circuit boards. When these are burned to release valuable materials, they also produce dangerous chemicals such as dioxins.

Energy

Computers use energy. Data centres use lots of energy. Much of this energy is used to run air-conditioning systems to cool the computers. It makes sense to reduce the energy used by computer systems. Methods include:

● virtual servers that reduce the number of physical servers in a data centre

● solid state storage that uses less energy than rotating disk drives

● automatic standby switching that turns computers off when they are not in use

● laying out equipment so that it can be cooled efficiently

● setting the air conditioning at an optimum level – not too low

● modern screens that are less energy intensive than the old CRT monitors.

Exam tip

Compare the good and bad effects of computers on the environment.

1　State two reasons why the disposal of obsolete computers is an environmental problem.　　*(2 marks)*

2　State two ways in which energy can be saved in a data centre.　　*(2 marks)*

Go online for answers　　　　　　　　　　　　　Online

Chapter 2 Computer hardware

Hardware is the term that describes the physical components of a computer system – anything that can be seen or touched.

Hardware components include **input, output, storage** and **processing** devices.

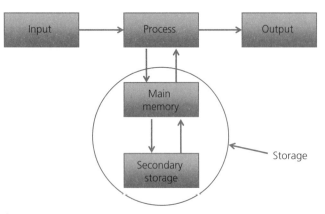

⬆ Figure 2.1 Hardware components of a system

Computer architecture

The architecture is the internal logical structure and organisation of the computer hardware.

The von Neumann architecture is the basis for all modern digital computers.

All data and instructions are stored in RAM, as **binary** numbers.

The central processing unit   Revised ☐

The central processing unit (CPU) carries out all the processing in a computer:

● The **arithmetic and logic unit (ALU)** carries out all of the arithmetic and logical operations.

● The **control unit** uses electrical signals to control the flow of data within the CPU.

The fetch–execute cycle

1 **Fetch** the instruction from memory.

2 **Decode** the instruction to find out what processing to do.

3 **Execute** the instruction.

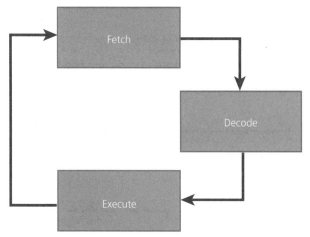

⬆ Figure 2.2 The fetch–execute cycle

The boot sequence

The **boot sequence** is a sequence of processes that contains all the information and instructions to get the computer up and running. It contains the **boot loader**, a program that starts this sequence when the computer is switched on.

After the boot sequence is completed, control is handed to the **operating system** to provide the programs for the CPU to process.

The speed at which a CPU can process data depends on:

- the CPU clock speed (processor speed)
- cache memory
- the number of processor cores.

Exam tip

Questions on these topics often require you to know these definitions.

CPU clock speed

The **speed** of the fetch–execute cycle is determined by an electronic clock chip.

The clock speed is measured in cycles per second, known as **hertz (Hz)**.

Processor speeds are typically measured in **gigahertz (GHz)**, billions of cycles per second.

Cache memory

The CPU cannot access main memory at the same speed as the processor clock chip; transferring data from main memory causes significant delays.

Cache memory has access times similar to the CPU but is **very expensive**.

A typical computer may well have 8 GB (gigabytes) of main memory but only 2 MB (megabytes) of cache memory.

Data that is in use is transferred to cache memory to make access to it faster.

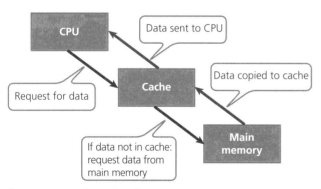

↑ **Figure 2.3 The role of cache memory in data transfer**

Multiple processor cores

Multi-core processors use multiple CPUs working together.

The CPUs can all fetch, decode and execute instructions at the same time.

The **advantage** is that more data is processed simultaneously.

The **disadvantage** is that more complicated operating systems are needed to manage them.

Exam tip

You need to know how all of these factors work together to affect how quickly the computer works.

Check your understanding

1 What is the purpose of the CPU? (1 mark)

2 What is meant by '2.5 MHz quad core' when describing a processor? (4 marks)

3 State one advantage and one disadvantage of a dual-core processor over a single-core processor. (2 marks)

Go online for answers

Memory

Random access memory (RAM)	Read only memory (ROM)
Volatile (data is lost when the power is turned off)	Non-volatile (data is retained when the power is turned off)
Can be accessed and changed by the computer at any time	Programmed during computer manufacture
Stores programs and data being used by the computer	Stores instructions and data required to start up the computer
Contains the operating system	Contains the boot program
Large (4 GB or more in a typical computer)	Small (1 or 2 MB required for the boot program)

Virtual memory

Virtual memory is part of the hard drive used as an extension to RAM. It is used when the computer does not have enough RAM to hold all the data and programs required.

Data is passed between RAM and virtual memory – access to virtual memory is slower than to RAM.

Adding more RAM reduces the use of virtual memory and improves the performance of the computer.

> **Exam tip**
>
> The way virtual and main memory interact and the effect this has on processing speed is important.

Check your understanding

1 Why does a computer have both ROM and RAM? (2 marks)

2 What is in RAM when the computer is working? (3 marks)

3 How does the use of virtual memory affect the performance of a computer? (3 marks)

4 How would installing extra RAM affect the use of virtual memory and what effect does this have on the performance of the computer? (2 marks)

Go online for answers

Flash memory

Flash memory is a type of ROM that can be rewritten.

Flash memory is used as a portable medium for storing and transferring data.

Advances in processor technology, mobile internet access and low power, high-capacity storage such as solid-state drives has led to technological convergence between mobile telephones and computers.

↑ Figure 2.4 USB memory stick

↑ Figure 2.6 Solid state drive (used in portable computers)

↑ Figure 2.5 Memory cards (used in cameras)

Binary logic

Revised

All computers work in binary and use simple **logic circuits** to make calculations.

The three main **logic gates** used are:

Input	Output
0	1
1	0

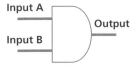

↑ Figure 2.7 NOT logic gate

Input A	Input B	Output
0	0	0
0	1	0
1	0	0
1	1	1

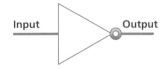

↑ Figure 2.8 AND logic gate

Input A	Input B	Output
0	0	0
0	1	1
1	0	1
1	1	1

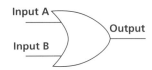

↑ Figure 2.9 OR logic gate

Exam tip

You will be expected to be able to:
- complete a truth table for a logic circuit
- draw a logic circuit defined using Boolean algebra.

Logic gates can be combined to make more complex circuits. The circuit in Figure 2.10 is **NOT(A AND B)**.

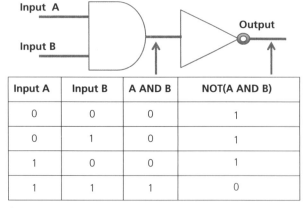

Input A	Input B	A AND B	NOT(A AND B)
0	0	0	1
0	1	0	1
1	0	0	1
1	1	1	0

↑ **Figure 2.10 NOT(A AND B) circuit**

Computers use binary values because it is easy to tell the state of a switch: on/off or 0/1.

The von Neumann principle is the foundation of modern digital computing. It uses binary values to store both data and instructions.

Data and instructions are indistinguishable from each other and are stored together in RAM.

Check your understanding   Tested

1 Determine the output from each of the following logic circuits:

a)   P   (1 mark)

b)   Q   (1 mark)

c)   R   (1 mark)

d)   S   (1 mark)

e)   T   (1 mark)

f)   V   (1 mark)

2 Copy and complete the truth table for the circuit in Figure 2.11. *(16 marks)*

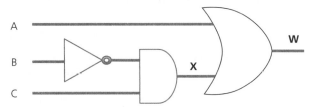

↑ **Figure 2.11 A complex logic circuit**

A	B	C	X	W
0	0	0		
0	0	1		
0	1	0		
0	1	1		
1	0	0		
1	0	1		
1	1	0		
1	1	1		

Go online for answers ────────────────────────── Online

Input and output devices ───────────────── Revised

Computers are used to process data we supply in order to provide us with the required output. A computer is of little value if it cannot accept inputs and provide outputs. There are many ways data can be input to or output from a computer. Some of these are:

Input devices

● Keyboard: used for data entry into a computer.

↑ **Figure 2.12 A keyboard**

● Mouse: controls a pointer on screen that can be opened, dragged or controlled by clicking buttons on the mouse.

↑ **Figure 2.13 A mouse**

Exam tip

You will be expected to be able to choose and justify hardware for a range of situations including unusual ones you may not be familiar with.

If you have learned about hardware devices that are appropriate to the situation then include them, even if they are not listed here.

● Touch screen: allows the user to interact directly with icons or an on-screen keyboard to control the device.

↑ **Figure 2.14 A touch screen**

● Microphone: uses voice input for communication or to control the device.

● Camera: captures images or video, e.g. for video conferencing or facial recognition.

↑ **Figure 2.15 A microphone**   ↑ **Figure 2.16 A camera**

● Bar code scanner: reads light reflected back from a pattern of thin and thick lines that represent a product code or other identification number.

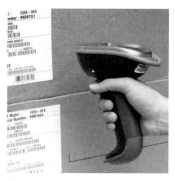

↑ **Figure 2.17 A bar code scanner**

● RFID reader: reads data from an electronic version of a bar code; does not require line of sight; it is used:

  ● in shops to identify products

  ● in airports to track luggage

  ● to tag animals

  ● to collect payments automatically in toll booths

  ● to access car parks.

- Sensor: detects physical conditions and automatically collects data:
  - temperature sensor
  - water level sensor
  - light sensor
  - pressure sensor
  - accelerometer
  - motion sensor.

- Eye-typer: can be used by people with limited physical mobility:
  - A camera tracks the movement of the user's eye and can detect which key the user is looking at.
  - A slow blink is used to select the key to type commands into a computer system.

- Foot mouse: can be used by people with limited hand movement; it is a track ball device that can be operated with the foot.

↑ **Figure 2.18 Foot mouse**

- Puff–suck switch: can be used by people with severely limited physical mobility by blowing into or sucking on a small tube.

↑ **Figure 2.19 Puff–suck switch**

- Braille keyboard: can be used by people with visual impairments to type text and commands into a computer system using keys with embossed patterns that match the standard Braille characters.

↑ **Figure 2.20 Braille keyboard**

Output devices

- Monitor: the most common way of displaying text, images and video:
  - LCD and LED monitors are most common.
  - Hand held devices have a touch screen display for input and output.

↑ **Figure 2.21 A monitor**

- Printer: produces hard copy on paper:
  - Monochrome or colour laser printers give fast economical output.
  - Inkjet printers give high-quality photographic images.
  - 3D printers make three-dimensional objects.
  - Thermal printers are used in EPOS systems because they are low cost and quiet.

↑ **Figure 2.22 An inkjet printer**

↑ **Figure 2.23 A 3D printer**

- Plotter: reproduces large-scale engineering or architectural drawings.

↑ **Figure 2.24 A plotter**

- Speakers: produce sound output:
  - music
  - warning sounds
  - voice for communication
  - synthetic voice (created by software) for screen reader systems.

↑ **Figure 2.25 A speaker**

- Actuators: create physical movements in response to a computer command to control aeroplanes, wheelchairs and robots.

↑ **Figure 2.26 An actuator**

Check your understanding
Tested

1 Identify two input devices and two output devices on a mobile phone. *(4 marks)*

2 Identify, with reasons, three devices that would help a visually impaired person to use a computer. *(6 marks)*

Go online for answers
Online

Secondary storage

Secondary storage is needed to store data and programs when the power is switched off.

Magnetic hard disk

A magnetic hard disk stores the operating system, installed programs and user data. Hard disks are:

- reliable
- high capacity
- low cost.

↑ **Figure 2.27 Magnetic hard disk**

Optical disk

An optical disk is excellent for transferring files or distributing software. Optical disks are:

- good capacity
- low cost
- lightweight and portable.

A CD can store 700 MB and a DVD can store 4.7 GB.

↑ **Figure 2.28 Optical disk**

Flash memory

Flash memory consumes little power. It is:

- good capacity (but less maximum capacity than a hard disk)
- used in hand held devices
- more expensive than a hard disk.

↑ **Figure 2.29 Flash memory**

Main considerations when selecting storage

- Capacity – how much data does it need to hold?
- Speed – how quickly can data be transferred?
- Portability – does it need to be portable and move data from one system to another?
- Durability – does it need to be transported and if so is it easily damaged?
- Reliability – does it need to be able to be used over and over again without failing?

> **Exam tip**
>
> You should be able to justify the choice of secondary storage for a situation based on capacity, speed, durability, portability and reliability.

Check your understanding Tested

1 Why does a computer need secondary storage? *(2 marks)*

2 What is the most suitable type of secondary storage for:

   a) transferring work between home and school *(1 mark)*

   b) distributing a software application *(1 mark)*

   c) storing work and programs on a large school network *(1 mark)*

   d) storing images in a digital camera? *(1 mark)*

Go online for answers Online

Chapter 3 Software

Software is the term given to the **programs** we run on our computers. The programs are the stored sets of **instructions** that are given to the **processor** to carry out. Software also refers to the **data** that is used by the programs.

Dedicated systems have software installed on a chip of some sort. This software is specific to the job and is only changed when updated. For example, a washing machine embedded system is only ever going to run software to control a washing machine.

Multi-purpose computers such as laptops, tablet computers, desktop PCs and phones regularly run different programs according to the wishes of the user.

↑ Figure 3.1 A laptop computer

↑ Figure 3.2 A tablet computer

↑ Figure 3.3 A desktop PC

Multi-purpose computers store their software on a secondary storage medium such as

- a hard disk
- a memory stick
- an SD card
- an optical disk (DVD or CD).

↑ Figure 3.4 A hard disk

↑ Figure 3.5 An SD card

The programs are loaded into RAM when required and the instructions are sent one at a time to the processor for decoding and execution.

Software comes in various types. The classifications can overlap to some extent.

- **System software** controls the hardware.
- **Application software** handles the real-world jobs that users want to do.
- **Utility software** has limited functionality and is used to maintain computer systems.

Software is usually produced using a **programming language**. Some software is produced by an automatic software generator.

> **Exam tip**
>
> Make sure you know something about a range of different computers and how they store their software.

System software

This is the software that controls the hardware. Without system software, applications programmers would have to take into account the precise movement of data between locations. System software takes care of that so that applications programmers can concentrate on developing algorithms to solve the real-world problems that the user has.

System software acts as an intermediary between the application and the hardware:

- It hides the complexities of the hardware from the user and the application programmer.
- It allows the user to operate the computer without having to write programs.

The main part of system software is the **operating system**. The operating system is a set of programs that controls the hardware and lets users and applications work with the computer. At its heart is the **kernel** which is the part of the operating system that actually makes the hardware do things.

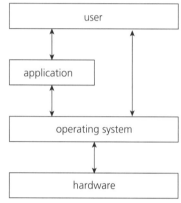

↑ **Figure 3.6 The software stack**

Check your understanding

1 State two reasons why an operating system is necessary in a computer. *(2 marks)*

2 Explain the relationship between an application and an operating system. *(2 marks)*

Go online for answers

User interface software

An operating system must provide a way for a user to control and interact with the computer. The user interface is the boundary between the human user and the machine. The interface:

- lets the user give commands
- asks questions
- displays a response.

Operating systems provide different ways of doing these things. New ways are constantly being developed.

Command-line interface

This interface requires the user to type commands. The commands are translated by a command interpreter into signals that the computer can understand. Figure 3.7 shows commands being typed into a Linux terminal.

```
sean@sean-Advent-4211:~$ ls
bin        Dropbox            Music      Templates  Ubuntu One
Desktop    examples.desktop   options    test2      Videos
Documents  hello              Pictures   test4      Xauthority.bak
Downloads  logfile            Public     test6
sean@sean-Advent-4211:~$ cal
   February 2013
Su Mo Tu We Th Fr Sa
                1  2
 3  4  5  6  7  8  9
10 11 12 13 14 15 16
17 18 19 20 21 22 23
24 25 26 27 28

sean@sean-Advent-4211:~$ w
 18:19:53 up 17 min,  2 users,  load average: 0.17, 0.43, 0.42
USER     TTY      FROM             LOGIN@   IDLE   JCPU   PCPU WHAT
sean     tty7                      18:02   17:10  40.93s  0.66s gnome-session -
sean     pts/0    :0               18:16    1.00s  0.96s  0.01s w
sean@sean-Advent-4211:~$ pwd
/home/sean
```

↑ **Figure 3.7 Commands in a Linux terminal**

The commands shown in Figure 3.7 are:

Command	Meaning	What it does
ls	list	Shows files in the current directory. Data files, executables and directories are colour coded in some systems.
cal	calendar	Shows the days of the current month (the command can be modified to show any month or any year).
w	who	Shows who is logged in and what are they doing.
pwd	present working directory	Shows the full location of your current directory.

You don't need to know these exact commands for the exam, but you should know that you can completely control a computer system with commands like these, which is why technicians and programmers like using them. They also find it useful to group commands like these together in **shell scripts**, to carry out maintenance jobs automatically. A **shell** is software that a user needs to communicate with the **kernel**.

Figure 3.8 shows a simple shell script that iterates through all the files in a directory and displays them.

```
#!/bin/bash
        for i in $( ls -l ); do
            echo item: $i
        done
```

↑ **Figure 3.8 Shell script**

Graphical User Interface (GUI)

A GUI uses images, known as **icons**, to represent resources, files, programs and actions. The user either clicks on areas of the screen with the mouse or touches or pinches them to make things happen. GUIs are a useful way to interact with a computer because:

● They are intuitive.

● No special training is required.

● Keyboard use is limited – useful where there is a small or virtual keyboard.

● No commands need to be learned.

Figure 3.9 shows a typical GUI that interacts with the Linux kernel.

↑ **Figure 3.9 A Linux GUI**

This interface sits on top of the operating system kernel and allows easy access to many of its everyday features such as:

● selecting software

● selecting files

● sending messages

● controlling sound volume

● connecting to WiFi

● deleting files

● moving files

● checking battery state

● updating software

● installing new software.

Touch screens

Some interfaces are designed for phones or tablets. These are not designed for mouse input but various actions of the fingers such as pinch, drag or tap.

↑ Figure 3.10 A touch screen interface

Natural language and speech

Some interfaces accept normal speech as input. This is a difficult thing to get right because speech can vary according to:

● accent
● speed of talking
● dialect used
● clarity of diction.

Speech input is useful for:

● selecting options on telephone menus
● giving commands to a computer
● dictating text.

The production of subtitles on television programmes involves speech recognition software. The difficulties can cause mistakes to be made.

↑ Figure 3.11 Television subtitles created by speech recognition software

1 List three maintenance actions that can be achieved with a typical operating system GUI. *(1 mark)*

2 Explain why voice input is still an underdeveloped area for user interface development. *(3 marks)*

3 Define the term 'user interface'. *(2 marks)*

4 Explain why computer technicians often use the command line in order to carry out system maintenance. *(3 marks)*

5 Explain the advantages of using a GUI to interact with a phone. *(3 marks)*

Go online for answers ──────────────────────────────── Online

Memory management ──────────────────────────────── Revised

Operating systems have to decide what goes where in memory. They have to make sure that:

● memory is used efficiently

● important data is not overwritten during the running of a program.

To do this, memory is divided into **pages**.

A program, when it is being executed, is called a **process**.

When a job needs to be done, the process is loaded into a vacant page. The operating system keeps track of this and protects it from being overwritten by other processes.

Virtual memory

Sometimes there are more jobs than there is space in memory to hold them. The operating system then swaps jobs in and out of memory, using a technique called **virtual memory**.

Virtual memory means 'not real' memory. It uses secondary storage (the disk) to hold parts of a program that are not currently needed. It is slower to access than main memory. A large program may take up too much memory so it is divided into modules.

● The modules are stored separately on secondary storage.

● When a module is needed, it is loaded into memory (swapped in) and run as a process.

● When a different module is needed, it can overwrite an unused module.

The operating system must keep track of which pages are vacant and which processes are currently swapped in or out.

Peripheral management

A **file** is a named store of data on a secondary storage medium.

Files can be:

● **data files**, such as a word processed document or a database

● **program files**, such as operating system components or applications

● **configuration data**, such as the parts of the Windows registry.

The operating system is responsible for keeping track of all files in a system. These are stored on secondary storage. They are copied into main memory when needed.

The operating system must know exactly where these files are located on the storage medium.

When you save a file, the operating system looks up where there is free space on the medium. It writes the data to the medium and makes a record of where it is located. Next time you need the file, the operating system looks up its location, finds it and retrieves it.

Fragmentation and defragmentation

Just as with main memory, secondary storage is divided into **segments**. Files are often larger than the size of a segment. So, files are usually split into **blocks** across many segments. These segments might be anywhere on the storage medium. If a file is split across many locations, it takes longer to read and write it. Each block contains information (**pointers**) about the location of the next block, so the operating system can follow the pointers to recover the whole file.

After a while, access to the files slows down. A process called **defragmentation** can then be used to tidy up the disk or other medium so that the parts of the files are moved to be stored next to each other.

Device drivers

The operating system has to take control of all the input to and output from a system. New input and output devices have to be accommodated. The manufacturers of equipment provide **device drivers**. A device driver is software that:

● creates an interface so that programmers do not need to be concerned about the peculiarities of the device

● allows an operating system to communicate with the device

● allows devices to operate independently of each other.

Multitasking

Most all-purpose systems commonly have several programs loaded into memory at the same time. This is called **multiprogramming**. Remember, when the program is being executed, it is called a **process**. In many cases, it seems to the user that the processes are running at the same time – this is called **multitasking**. For example, we can carry on with our work while a document prints or a file is downloading from the internet. In reality, these things do not happen at the same time. The operating system shifts its attention between processes, often so fast that the user doesn't notice.

A multiprogramming operating system must:

● make sure that the CPU is in use as much of the time as possible

● try to speed up the operation of all tasks

● share resources fairly between tasks.

When there are several processes sharing the single processor, the operating system uses a **scheduler** in order to allocate time. The allocation is made according to a policy. This policy might be:

● shortest job first

● round robin – all jobs get equal time

Exam tip

It is important to be able to give details in your answers:

● You should be able to say something about how a defragmenter or other process works.

● You should be able to state several distinct jobs performed by an operating system.

Slow down and read the questions really carefully and answer the points wanted, not the points you wanted to answer.

- first come first served
- priorities – some jobs are more important than others, for example when the user is making inputs, a virus scan might be relegated to a background task.

Exam tip

As always, learn some details. Giving some examples is often worth extra marks.

Files and directories

Revised

File systems

Operating systems organise files on secondary storage. Most use hierarchical systems:

- Files are stored in directories.
- Directories can include subdirectories.

A **directory** is a logical grouping of files. In Windows systems, directories are called **folders**. Directories are useful because they:

- make it easier for a human user to locate related files
- allow the repeated use of the same file name in different locations.

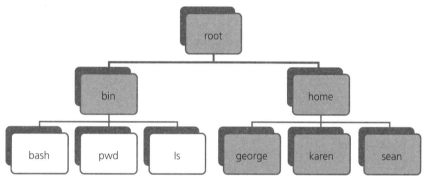

↑ **Figure 3.12 A hierarchical directory structure (directories are shown in green, files in white)**

File extensions

Some file systems use file **extensions**. These are parts of the file name that indicate what type of file it is. In Windows systems, the file extension is given after a dot. Examples are:

Extension	Meaning
doc	Word document
pdf	Portable document format – used for storing documents in exactly defined format
html	Hypertext markup language – used for web pages
xls	Microsoft Excel spreadsheet
mdb	Microsoft Access database
exe	Executable – a program that can be run
jpg	Joint Photographic Experts Group – a compressed image file format
mp3	Moving Pictures Expert Group Audio Layer 3 – a common music file format using lossy compression

Attributes

Files can be given different **attributes**, which provide extra information about the file, such as:

- who created the file
- who can view it or edit it

Exam tip

These file extensions are just *some* examples. You don't necessarily have to learn these examples. Just be able to quote *some* examples.

- whether it is read-only
- whether it is hidden
- date it was last accessed
- date it was last changed
- size of the file
- whether it has been backed up (archive flag).

Check your understanding   Tested

1 Explain what file attributes are.   (2 *marks*)
2 State three common file attributes.   (3 *marks*)
3 Explain what is meant by a file system.   (2 *marks*)

Go online for answers   Online

Security   Revised

Viruses

Viruses are programs that replicate themselves. They attach themselves to legitimate programs. They often have a payload which is designed to do such things as:

- damage files
- take control of a computer
- retrieve confidential data.

Some viruses have no payload but can still cause damage.

Some operating systems, such as Windows, allow users and viruses high levels of privilege. Unix and Linux systems are more tightly controlled so viruses are much less of a problem.

Authentication

Operating systems usually allow the authentication of users. This means they can be set up to check that users are who they say they are. This normally involves users having:

- a user id: this checks who they are and what privileges they have
- a password: this confirms that they really are who they say they are.

Privileges

Privileges are the rights assigned to users and groups. They may include features such as whether for a particular file the user can:

- read (view it)
- write (change it)
- execute (run it if it is a program).

Encryption

Some files are encrypted. That is they are transformed in such a way that an unauthorised person cannot understand them. It is common for user passwords to be stored in an encrypted state.

> **Exam tip**
>
> Make sure you know about file permissions and that access to files can be controlled.

1 Explain what user privileges are. *(2 marks)*

2 Explain how an operating system determines a user's privileges. *(2 marks)*

Go online for answers — Online

Programming software — Revised

Editors

Editors or **text editors** are like cut-down word processors. They allow text files to be:

● created

● saved

● read

● changed.

They do not save extra characters such as formatting information.

They are particularly useful for writing the source code of programs and editing configuration files.

All operating systems come with a variety of editors as standard.

Examples of editors are:

● Notepad (Windows)

● Notepad (Yahoo)

● vi (Unix)

● nano (Unix equivalents).

Linkers

These combine modules of **object code** (compiled program code) into a single executable program.

Interpreters

These convert typed commands into the machine instructions that the processor understands.

Applications and utilities — Revised

Applications are the programs that people use to do real-world jobs. There are huge numbers of them and they include such examples as:

● word processors

● autopilots

● traffic light controls

● payroll processing

● hotel booking systems

● train lookup programs

● bar code readers

● MP3 players

● games

● engine management systems.

> **Exam tip**
>
> Make a quick list of some applications that you have used recently.

Utilities are software tools that help make maintaining the system easier. Most operating systems come bundled with lots of utilities. Here are some common ones:

- Antivirus utilities detect and remove viruses (remember that viruses are self-replicating programs).

- Spyware protection checks for and removes programs that record the websites you visit and the passwords you use.

- Firewalls monitor traffic entering and leaving a system in order to block unauthorised material.

- Disk organisation utilities include:

  - Formatting – prepares new media for receiving data.

  - File transfer – copies files from one location to another. FTP utilities are for copying files across a network.

  - Defragmentation – reorganises files that have been split on secondary storage. It relocates the fragments close together so that access is faster.

- System maintenance utilities help you to clear away redundant files, update registry entries and check for missing dependencies.

- System information and diagnosis utilities, such as Windows scandisk, check for problems on secondary storage. Others can report disk and memory usage.

- System cleanup tools, such as Ccleaner, search for unused files and clear them out. They can be used to remove internet cache files, cookies and history files.

- Automatic updating utilities check online for updates at intervals. The updates are to fix bugs or security loopholes. New features may be added. Some systems automatically make the updates, others ask first. Virus checkers often update regularly.

↑ **Figure 3.13 Software updater dialog**

↑ **Figure 3.14 System utilities**

Check your understanding ————————————————————————— Tested

1 List three common utilities supplied with most operating systems. *(3 marks)*

2 Explain why many operating systems have automatic update features. *(3 marks)*

3 Explain what disk formatting is for. *(1 mark)*

Go online for answers ————————————————————————— Online

Software procurement ————————————————————————— Revised

Software can be obtained from various sources. Systems managers must make choices so that their organisation gets systems:

● as required

● that users will want to use

● on time

● at a reasonable cost

● of an acceptable quality.

Custom written software

Custom written software is software specially commissioned for a particular customer.

Advantages:

● It should have exactly the features required.

● It should not require special adaptations to be made after installation.

● A maintenance contract can be arranged with the developer.

● The developer can be contacted to solve issues.

● The developer may provide training.

Disadvantages:

● It may not have been extensively tested.

● It may be expensive as the developer has to make a profit from just one customer.

● It may take a long time to develop.

Off the shelf software

This is sometimes called 'shrink-wrapped' software. It can be bought from a supplier already boxed up and ready to install.

Examples include:

● Microsoft Office

● Windows

● Norton security software.

Advantages:

● It is ready immediately.

● It has probably been extensively tested.

● Many users will know about it and may have discovered and reported problems.

● There will be lots of forums online where users can help each other.

● The cost will be low because the developer costs are shared among many users.

Disadvantages:

- It probably won't be exactly what the customer needs.
- It may need extensive customisation.
- The customer might have to search for training providers.

Open source software

This is software that has been placed in the public domain by the programmers. They often produce software to improve their skills or for the public good. Some of the most widely used software in the world is open source.

Examples include:

- Linux
- Apache web server
- Libre Office
- Firefox.

Advantages:

- It may be free of charge.
- It can be altered because the source code is available.
- It may be extremely reliable and efficient because many people may work to improve it.

Disadvantages:

- There are no maintenance contracts.
- There is no one to contact if there are problems.
- Updates may not happen or come at irregular intervals.
- The software may be for a different platform than the company currently owns.

Proprietary software

This is software that is developed for profit by a company. The source code is retained as a valuable trade secret. Only the compiled code is released. Users buy a licence to use it.

Advantages:

- There is someone to go to if there is a problem.
- It should have been extensively tested.
- Updates are usually scheduled regularly.

Disadvantages:

- It can be expensive.
- Deliberate incompatibilities may be introduced so users can get locked in.
- It may be inflexible to users' needs.

> **Exam tip**
>
> As always, learn a few examples to quote in answers.

Check your understanding　　　　　　　　　　　　　　　　　　　**Tested**

1 State two advantages and two disadvantages of buying custom written software for an organisation.　　　　　　　　　　　　　　　*(4 marks)*

2 Explain what is meant by open source software.　　　　　　*(3 marks)*

Go online for answers　　　　　　　　　　　　　　　　　　　　**Online**

Chapter 4 Representing data

Numbers

Modern computers work in binary because it is easy to represent two states in simple electronic circuits.

● All **data** and **instructions** are in **binary**.

● Binary is a number system with just two symbols, 0 and 1.

● Each digit in a binary number is called a **bit** (**b**inary dig**it**).

Converting from binary to denary

The binary number system works like the familiar base 10 system using multiples of two, instead of ten, for column values. In binary the column values are:

128	64	32	16	8	4	2	1

If we want to know what the binary number 10110 is in **denary** (base 10) then we put this number into the table and add together the column values where there is a '1':

128	64	32	16	8	4	2	1	
			1	0	1	1	0	
			16		4	2		= 22

> **Exam tip**
>
> Draw these tables to show your working. Credit may be available even with one minor error.

Check your understanding

1   Convert 10110 to denary (base 10). *(1 mark)*

2   Convert 1001001 to denary (base 10). *(1 mark)*

3   Convert 11001101 to denary (base 10). *(1 mark)*

Go online for answers

Units

A group of 8 binary digits or bits is called a **byte**.

As in base 10 we have names for key values based on 2^{10} or 1024 bytes:

Value	Name
8 bits	1 byte
1024 bytes	1 kilobyte
1024 kilobytes	1 megabyte
1024 megabytes	1 gigabyte
1024 gigabytes	1 terabyte

Half a byte, 4 bits, is generally called a **nibble**.

Converting from denary to binary

One method for converting denary (base 10) to binary is repeated division by 2, recording the remainder each time.

For example, convert 205 base 10 into binary:

205	÷ 2	=	102	Remainder	1									
102	÷ 2	=	51	Remainder	0									
51	÷ 2	=	25	Remainder	1									
25	÷ 2	=	12	Remainder	1									
12	÷ 2	=	6	Remainder	0									
6	÷ 2	=	3	Remainder	0									
3	÷ 2	=	1	Remainder	1									
1	÷ 2	=	0	Remainder	1									
							1	1	0	0	1	1	0	1

The answer is the remainder column starting at the last value, so 205 in base 10 = 11001101 in binary.

Some useful binary numbers are:

Base 10	Binary
1	1
2	10
3	11
4	100
5	101

Adding binary numbers

Adding in binary uses the same approach as in base 10: we add the values and if the value is larger than the column will hold we 'carry' a value to the next column.

To add 1101 to 1011 in binary:

		1	1	0	1
+		1	0	1	1
	1	1	0	0	0
Carried values	1	1	1	1	

1 + 1 = 10 (in binary)

    so we write 0 for the answer and carry 1

0 + 1 + 1 = 10

    so we write 0 and carry 1

1 + 0 + 1 = 10

    so we write 0 and carry 1

1 + 1 + 1 = 11

    so we write 1 and carry 1

0 + 1 = 1

    so we write 1

If a computer uses storage values that are 8 bits long and we add together 11000010 and 10111010, we find the following happens:

	1	1	0	0	0	0	1	0
+	1	0	1	1	1	0	1	0
1	0	1	1	1	1	1	0	0
1						1		

We need a ninth binary digit.

If our computer has only 8 bits to store a value then this last bit will be lost.

This is called **overflow**: The result of the addition is too big to fit in the available space.

> **Exam tip**
>
> Make sure you include the carry digits to show your working. Don't be tempted to convert to base 10 then add, but do check your answers afterwards by doing this.

Check your understanding — Tested

1 Add 101100 and 111001 in binary. *(2 marks)*

2 Add 101111 and 10011 in binary. *(2 marks)*

3 Add 1001101 and 101011 in binary. *(2 marks)*

Go online for answers — Online

Hexadecimal numbers — Revised

Large binary numbers are difficult to remember and programmers want something that is easily converted from binary but also easy to remember or recognise.

An 8-bit byte splits easily into two 4-bit nibbles.

128	64	32	16		8	4	2	1
8	4	2	1		8	4	2	1
These are now 16s								

In four bits, the largest value we can store is 1111 or 8 + 4 + 2 + 1 = 15.

If we are to represent each nibble using a single digit we need more symbols.

In hexadecimal we use the letters A to F to represent the base 10 numbers 10 to 15.

Base 10	Base 2	Base 16
0	0	0
1	1	1
2	10	2
3	11	3
4	100	4
5	101	5
6	110	6
7	111	7
8	1000	8
9	1001	9
10	1010	A
11	1011	B
12	1100	C
13	1101	D
14	1110	E
15	1111	F

Converting between hexadecimal and denary

Converting from **hex** (base 16) to denary (base 10) uses column values.

For example 27 hex in base 10 is:

16	1
2	7
$2 \times 16 = 32$	$7 \times 1 = 7$

$32 + 7 = 39$ in base 10.

Another example: convert BD in hex into base 10:

16	1
B	D
$11 \times 16 = 176$	$13 \times 1 = 13$

$176 + 13 = 189$ in base 10.

To convert from base 10 to hexadecimal, we can use the repeated division approach: divide by 16 and record the remainders until the result is 0.

Convert 197 in base 10 into hexadecimal:

197	÷ 16	=	12	Remainder	5		
12	÷ 16	=	0	Remainder	C		
						C	5

197 base 10 is C5 in hexadecimal.

Tested

Check your understanding

1   Convert 3A hexadecimal to denary (base 10).   *(2 marks)*
2   Convert AD hexadecimal to denary (base 10).   *(2 marks)*
3   Convert 5E hexadecimal to denary (base 10).   *(2 marks)*
4   Convert 91 base 10 to hexadecimal (base 16).   *(2 marks)*
5   Convert 169 base 10 to hexadecimal (base 16).   *(2 marks)*
6   Convert 51 base 10 to hexadecimal (base 16).   *(2 marks)*

Go online for answers   Online

Converting between hexadecimal and binary

This may seem a little tricky but consider converting between hexadecimal and binary.

To convert from binary to hex simply split the binary number into two nibbles and convert each one to get the hexadecimal equivalent.

Convert 10100011 (binary) to hexadecimal:

8	4	2	1		8	4	2	1
1	0	1	0		0	0	1	1
10 in base 10 = A hex					3 in base 10 = 3 hex			

So 10100011 is A3 in hexadecimal.

To convert from hexadecimal to binary we simply replace each hex digit with the equivalent binary nibble.

● Convert BD (hex) to a binary number:

   B (hex) = 11 (base 10) = 1011 (binary)

   D (hex) = 13 (base 10) = 1101 (binary)

   BD in hex is 10111101 in binary.

● Convert C5 (hex) to a binary number:

   C (hex) = 12 (base 10) = 1100 (binary)

   5 (hex) = 5 (base 10) = 0101 (binary)

   C5 in hex is 11000101 in binary.

Check your understanding   Tested

1   Convert 10110110 binary to hex (base 16).   *(2 marks)*
2   Convert 11001001 binary to hex (base 16).   *(2 marks)*
3   Convert 10011011 binary to hex (base 16).   *(2 marks)*
4   Convert A5 hexadecimal to binary.   *(2 marks)*
5   Convert 7D hexadecimal to binary.   *(2 marks)*
6   Convert F3 hexadecimal to binary.   *(2 marks)*

Go online for answers   Online

Characters

- All the symbols displayed by a computer are represented by a code.
- The computer looks up the symbol matching the code from a list of codes and their associated characters.
- The list of codes and matching characters is the **character set** for the computer.
- The codes used are stored in binary.
- The number of bits used to store the code determines how many characters or symbols can be used.
- ASCII uses 7 bits so can provide 127 characters or symbols plus the null character (128 in total).
- Extended ASCII uses 8 bits making it possible to use 256 characters or symbols in total.
- Unicode uses 16 bits, providing over 65 000 possibilities, or 32 bits providing over 4 billion possibilities.
- Unicode can provide a character set for a computer that includes a wide range of specialist symbols.
- Unicode keeps the same assignment of codes for the original 127 ASCII codes so ASCII could now be considered a subset of Unicode.

Some ASCII codes:

Binary	Hex	Decimal	Character
0100000	20	32	space
1000001	41	65	A
1000010	42	66	B
1011010	5A	90	Z
1100001	61	97	a
1111001	79	121	y
1111010	7A	122	z
1111111	7F	127	delete

ASCII codes for characters increase from 'A' to 'Z' and from 'a' to 'z':

- Characters can be sorted on their numeric code values.
- If characters are sorted, 'Z' comes before 'a' because of its ASCII value.
- When we sort words 'Zebra' comes before 'apple'.

Check your understanding

1 What happens if you sort the list 'Gorilla', 'bear', 'Elephant', 'Cat', 'dog' in a computer program using ASCII or Unicode to represent the character set? *(2 marks)*

2 What is the difference between using the ASCII character set and the Unicode character set? *(2 marks)*

Go online for answers

Online

Images

Images are stored in binary on a computer.

This image of flowers is stored as a lot of binary values:

⬆ **Figure 4.1 A digital photograph and the binary values stored in its file**

The computer is able to work out how to turn these binary values into the image because the file with the binary data contains **metadata** (data about the data).

The metadata for this image is shown in Figure 4.2:

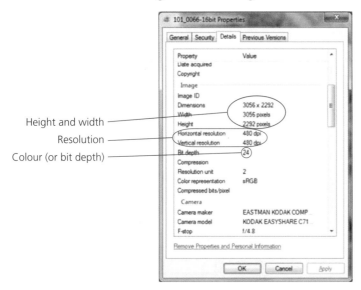

Height and width
Resolution
Colour (or bit depth)

⬆ **Figure 4.2 Metadata for a digital photograph**

The height and width of the image are measured in pixels:

- A **pixel** is one 'dot' in the image.
- The number of bits we use for a pixel determines how many colours each dot can represent:
  - 1 bit can represent just two colours, i.e. black and white.
  - 2 bits can represent 2^2 or 4 colours.
  - 8 bits can represent 2^8 or 256 colours.
  - 16 bits can represent 2^{16} or 65 536 colours.
- The more bits per pixel (bpp) the greater the **colour depth** and the more bits we need to store the data.
  - 16 bpp is called high colour.
  - 24 bpp is called true colour.

- The **resolution** is the number of **pixels per unit**, for example, the number of pixels per inch (usually called dots per inch or dpi).
- The more pixels per inch, the more data to be stored and the larger the file needed to store the image.

If a **bitmapped image** is displayed enlarged on screen the actual image size does not change, the dots just get bigger and the image becomes **pixelated** or 'blocky'.

Exam tip

Be careful: the size of the displayed image and the size of the file image are not the same thing. An image may be displayed at an enlarged size on screen without changing the size of the file.

Check your understanding ──────────────────── Tested ☐

1 How many colours can be represented using a 4-bit colour depth? *(1 mark)*
2 Figure 4.2 shows the metadata for the image of the flowers. What is:
   a) the size of the image
   b) the colour depth of the image
   c) the resolution of the image? *(3 marks)*
3 What are the main factors affecting the size of the file needed to store an image? *(3 marks)*

Go online for answers ──────────────────── Online ☐

Sound ──────────────────── Revised ☐

Sound files are described by **metadata** to make sure the computer can interpret the data accurately.

The data stored includes the **audio codec** and the **sample rate**.

Sound is an **analogue** (continuously varying) form so to transfer sound to a computer it needs to be digitally sampled.

The **sample interval** is often used to describe the sample rate and is the time between samples being taken – the higher the sample interval the lower the sample rate.

When sound is sampled at a low rate:

- Very few samples are taken.
- There is a poor match between the original sound and the sampled sound.
- A small file size is required.

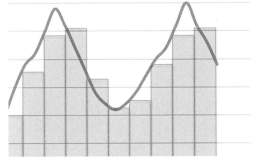

↑ **Figure 4.3 Sound sampled at a low rate**

When sound is sampled at a higher rate:

● Many more samples are taken.

● There is a good match between the original sound and the sampled sound.

● A large file size is required.

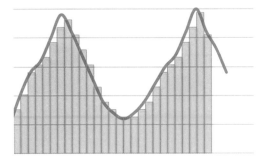

↑ **Figure 4.4 Sound sampled at a high rate**

The **bit rate** is the amount of space used for each sample.

A high bit rate means:

● more accurate sampling at each point which gives better quality

● more data needs to be stored which needs a larger file size.

A typical MP3 track is stored at 128 kbits per second.

An audio CD uses 1411.2 kbits per second.

Exam tip

Don't confuse sample rate and bit rate; they are different. The sample rate is how frequently the data is sampled; the bit rate is the amount of data stored at each sample point.

Check your understanding — Tested

1 How does sample rate affect the quality of the playback for an MP3 sound track? *(2 marks)*

2 What factors affect the file size for a sampled MP3 sound track? *(4 marks)*

Go online for answers — Online

Instructions — Revised

When a computer is instructed to run a program it is directed to a specific location in memory that contains the first instruction in the program.

The CPU **fetches** this instruction and decodes it in order to find out what to do next.

The instruction is in two parts:

● **operator**: the instruction part

● **operand**: the data part.

For example, if the first location contains:

1	0	0	1	1	0	1	1

This will be split into two parts:

1	0	0	1

Operator

1	0	1	1

Operand

The operator binary code (opcode) represents an operation; for example, 1001 may mean 'ADD the contents of the operand to the accumulator'.

The operand represents the data that the operator uses; in this case, the program adds the value it finds in memory location 1011 to the value in the accumulator.

The **accumulator** is a special register in the CPU used to store the results of any calculation.

The CPU cannot tell the difference between data and instructions and simply deals with what it finds according to what it expects to find.

Check your understanding

Tested

1   How does a computer tell the difference between instructions and data?   *(2 marks)*

2   How are instructions stored in binary in a computer?   *(2 marks)*

Go online for answers

Online

Chapter 5 Databases

A database is a **persistent organised** store of data on a computer system.

● persistent – it is saved on secondary storage for the future

● organised – databases have a structure so that they can be easily processed.

The importance of databases

Most organisations depend on their databases in order to operate properly. In many cases, businesses could not function without them. Because of this, databases need to be:

● accurate

● up to date

● available to those who need to use them

● protected from those who should not have access.

Database administrators go to great lengths in order to protect their data against:

● errors

● loss

● insufficient data

● inconsistencies

● unauthorised access.

Errors in databases can result in:

● embarrassment, such as sending bills to customers who have died

● financial loss, such as if a bank account is wrongly credited or debited

● life or death situations, such as incorrect navigational data for aircraft.

> **Exam tip**
> Be aware of how important databases are. You should always be prepared for questions about them.

> **Exam tip**
> You should know some examples of how database problems are avoided.
> Be aware of some of the problems that can result from errors in databases.

Data security and data integrity

Revised

Data **security** refers to keeping data safe. It is important that data is not lost, otherwise a business might not be able to function. Data can be lost because of:

● a catastrophe, such as fire or flood

● an accident, such as an employee deleting data

● malicious action, such as by an intruder.

Data is protected against loss by:

● making regular backups

● having a mirror database server so that data is saved in at least two places

● storing backups in a safe place such as in the cloud or otherwise off site

● restricting access

● keeping audit trails of who has accessed data.

Data **integrity** means that the data reflects reality. It implies that the data is correct and fit for purpose. Data integrity can be maximised by:

● suitable validation

● software that prevents inconsistent states.

Validation

Validation is the process of checking data when it is input. Validation is carried out by software, not by humans. It checks that data conforms to certain rules. Here are some examples.

Exam tip

Remember that validation can be set up in any way that the database designer wants. It is not just limited to the examples here.

Validation method	Meaning	Example of use
Length check	Must have a certain number of characters or be above or below some limit.	A password must be long enough to be strong.
Type check	Must be a certain data type such as character or number.	No numerals allowed in a surname.
Range check	Must fall between certain limits.	Date of birth for a job applicant.
Presence check	Must be filled in.	Surname when applying for a job.
Lookup check	Must match what is held on file.	Check that a password is correct.
Format check	Must conform to a certain pattern.	Car registration number must be LLNNLLL (L = letter, N = number).
Check digit	Must be exactly the same as data previously entered. An algorithm calculates an extra digit which is appended to the data. The same algorithm checks data when input.	ISBN (International Book Number).

Verification

Verification is checking that the data entered is correct. It can be a simple visual check against the source data or an algorithm checks two copies, entered independently, and flags up inconsistencies.

Check your understanding
Tested

1 Explain the term 'validation'. *(3 marks)*

2 What is meant by a range check? *(2 marks)*

3 Explain the term 'verification'. *(2 marks)*

4 What is a check digit? *(2 marks)*

5 A data table is set up to hold personal details of customers for an online business. Describe how the following fields would be validated:

  a) surname *(2 marks)*

  b) date of birth *(2 marks)*

  c) gender *(2 marks)*

  d) credit limit *(2 marks)*

  e) telephone number *(2 marks)*

  f) password. *(2 marks)*

6 Here is part of a database of customer details:

Holden	Keely	6133 Donec Rd.	Birmingham
Swanson	Roanna	572 Hendrerit. Road	Birmingham
Stark	Anthony	4924 At Ave	Cheltenham
Hughes	Norman	Ap #703-3873 Quisque Rd.	Worcester
Saunders	Vivian	575-4103 Libero. Ave	Cheltenhm
Hooper	Aimee	7860 Augue Road	B'ham

a) Define the term data redundancy. *(1 mark)*

b) Explain how data redundancy affects this table. *(2 marks)*

c) Explain what problems might occur as a result of the redundancy in this example. *(2 marks)*

d) Explain how the data could be stored to eliminate this problem. *(2 marks)*

Go online for answers ─────────────────────────── Online

Databases are everywhere ─────────────── Revised

It is hard to think of any organisation that does not make use of databases. Databases affect most aspects of our lives. Everyone has details about themselves stored on many databases.

Here are just a few examples of where databases are used:

Situation	Example of use
Telephone company	Customers, phone calls, payments, locations of masts
School	Students, exams, results, staff, inventories
Bank	Accounts, transactions, customers
Shops	Customers, prices, inventories, sales
Doctors	Patients, drugs, hospitals
Internet Service Providers	DNS data (IP addresses), router addresses, customers, usage information
Government	Tax records, drivers and vehicles
Airline booking agency	Flights, customers, bookings, airlines, airports

Database operations

Database administrators create and look after databases. They make use of database applications software. Every situation that uses a database needs special software to make the database useful and achieve the business objectives of an organisation.

Databases help organisations to process information. They make data easy to:

- access
- search
- sort
- group
- copy
- protect.

A subset of the data in a database is called a **view**. Making suitable views for each staff member increases the efficiency of using the database and reduces risks.

In an organisation, databases and their applications software give every member of staff the right information they need to do their jobs – enough and no more. Giving a user too much access increases the risks of damaging the data by accident or deliberately.

Standard operations on databases are sometimes listed under the term **CRUD**. This is an easy way to remember the basic things that most users need to do to a database:

● **C**reate

● **R**ead

● **U**pdate

● **D**elete.

Things are usually more complex than that. It is possible to apply all sorts of algorithms to data in order to gain additional benefits from databases.

Data matching compares different databases to look for particular relationships. For example, it can be used to compare housing benefit claims with credit agency data in order to uncover benefit fraud.

Data mining is a process that looks in many different unrelated databases. It may show up unexpected relationships that may not have been noticed before. An example is using supermarket loyalty card data to look for connections between purchases and various lifestyle indicators such as postcodes.

Data models

Revised

Databases are organised according to a **model**. A model is a **data structure** that attempts to represent reality in such a way that is useful to the owner of the database. For example, a hotel booking agency needs data organised around hotels, rooms, dates and customers.

Flat file database

The simplest model is a **flat file** database. This is just rows and columns such as would be suitable for an address book.

Each row is called a **record** and each column is called a **field**.

It is easy to set up a flat file database using just a spreadsheet.

	A	B	C	D	E	F
1	Surname	Forename	Address1	City	PostCode	Telephone
2	Hess	Marny	P.O. Box 380, 8135 Vel Street	DuBois	F41 4BZ	01 55 850 3559-1155
3	Mcdaniel	Micah	341-4797 Sit Street	Portsmouth	Y1 9JH	01 44 389 1304-9631
4	Savage	Silas	Ap #732-6465 Lacinia Road	Waltham	RB8P 1UZ	01 51 479 4834-2206
5	Harding	Thomas	105-7938 Tortor St.	West Sacramento	BP8X 2AR	01 24 852 7911-4335
6	Wynn	Rachel	7426 Sed. Rd.	Lake Charles	KK7 0GR	01 32 447 2999-9004
7	Hurst	Jin	407-9261 Ac Rd.	Burlington	U7 8FO	01 84 306 6448-4374
8	Jenkins	Tanek	797-3977 Sed Avenue	Nome	T1 7NZ	01 57 531 8484-9224
9	Moon	Ahmed	7332 Erat St.	Auburn Hills	L96 7RV	01 52 809 4301-8957
10	Cobb	Otto	557 Eu. Av.	Vincennes	ZY2 4WX	01 25 767 5668-0798
11	Osborne	Judah	P.O. Box 811, 6986 Pretium Av.	Worland	QP5P 8AL	01 81 958 7043-9419
12	Goodman	Regan	Ap #674-7616 Neque Avenue	Hampton	ZH2 5WC	01 62 972 4594-0245
13	Gould	Ezra	Ap #880-8212 Curabitur St.	Greenfield	ZF1 2LT	01 15 434 2687-5377
14	Rivera	Freya	P.O. Box 357, 8026 Vitae St.	Boston	S2 1YM	01 43 349 6837-4249
15	Mcdowell	Demetrius	Ap #925-4580 Magna. Road	Scranton	X34 6PN	01 60 992 4882-2674
16	Bright	Oren	Ap #469-9500 Pulvinar Road	Jeffersonville	QD6Y 5IO	01 19 698 9377-6943
17	Holden	Keely	6133 Donec Rd.	Texarkana	TP6W 2PK	01 61 557 4468-1441
18	Swanson	Roanna	572 Hendrerit. Road	Frankfort	DO6 7FO	01 18 969 4278-6467
19	Stark	Anthony	4924 At Ave	Claremore	MH46 8DK	01 17 496 2803-6890
20	Hughes	Norman	Ap #703-3873 Quisque Rd.	Burbank	RI4D 9HH	01 43 972 6916-2741

↑ **Figure 5.1 A flat file database**

Flat file databases are very limited. One of their main problems is that data might be repeated unnecessarily, such as in the names of cities in an address book. Unnecessary repetition of data is called **data redundancy**. This can lead to inconsistent spellings which can cause problems when searching for data. It also leads to inconsistent updates. Some occurrences of a data item might be updated and others might not.

Hierarchical database

A **hierarchical** model is sometimes useful when making an inventory. Some parts of stock items might always belong with others.

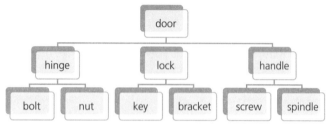

↑ **Figure 5.2 A hierarchical database**

Relational database

Relational databases are the most useful model and consequently the most common type of database. They are far more flexible than other models and can replace other models in most cases.

Relational databases store their data in separate tables. The tables are linked together so that related data can easily be extracted.

Each **table** in a relational database contains data about an **entity**. An entity is something in real life about which we store data. It might be a customer, an invoice or a restaurant booking. The whole point about thinking in terms of entities is that data should be stored once only. That way, you know you are always looking at the single up-to-date version.

Most well-designed relational databases separate data so that entities are linked in one-to-many relationships. This means that one member of a table (a record) might have links with many members of a different table.

You can show this relationship with a crow's foot 'entity–relationship' diagram like this:

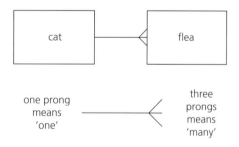

↑ **Figure 5.3 An entity–relationship diagram**

Figure 5.3 shows two entities, cats and fleas. One cat can have many fleas but each flea only has one cat.

Here is an entity–relationship diagram that shows the relationship between clients, bookings and rooms in a hotel booking system.

↑ **Figure 5.4 Hotel booking entity–relationship diagram**

A room can be booked many times. A client may make many bookings. But a particular booking is for just one room for just one client.

The DBMS

A DBMS is a **Database Management System**. This is software that looks after a database at a fundamental level. It is a general-purpose tool that allows database administrators to:

● create database applications

● protect data

● run queries to extract data

● keep data consistent

● keep data accurate.

Some DBMSs are small systems for personal computers. Others are huge systems that are designed for large organisations.

Separation of data and applications

The DBMS acts as a go-between, connecting applications to the underlying data.

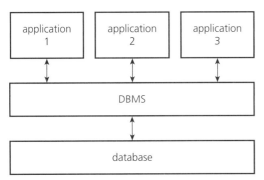

↑ **Figure 5.5 Separation of data and applications**

It is important to separate the applications from the data so that:

● Programmers do not have to worry that their applications might damage existing data structures.

● New applications can be written without restructuring the data.

● Data can be more easily shared between applications.

● Data remains consistent because there is just one copy for all applications.

Transactions

When a change takes place in a database, it is called a **transaction**. Transactions must not damage the integrity of a database.

Imagine a transfer of money between two different accounts in a bank. Suppose one account is debited but another is not credited. This would mean that the overall state of the database – the total amount of money in the system – would be different after the transaction. The database has become inconsistent. The data no longer reflects reality – it has lost integrity.

A DBMS has features that protect data integrity.

Multi-user databases

Most commercial databases are multi-user. Many people need to access them at the same time. This can cause conflicts. If two users try to modify data at the same time, one of the transactions will fail. To avoid this, most DBMSs use **record locking**. This means that if one user has opened a record for writing (editing), other users can only view it until the transaction is committed. Then it is unlocked for other users.

Check your understanding — Tested

1　Explain what a DBMS is. *(3 marks)*

2　What is a database? *(3 marks)*

3　What is a flat file database? *(1 mark)*

4　Explain what a relational database is. *(3 marks)*

Go online for answers — Online

Common tools provided by a DBMS — Revised

Most database management systems have a set of standard tools. You can see them in such products as Microsoft Access or Libre Office Base. The following examples are based on a hotel booking database.

Tables

These are the structures where data is stored. The DBMS provides tools for creating and modifying tables.

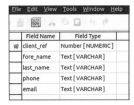

↑ **Figure 5.6 Database table**

● Each table contains data about just one entity.

● A row is equivalent to a record.

● Each row in a table is made up in the same way – it has the same fields and all rows are the same size.

- Each table has a primary key:
  - A primary key uniquely identifies a record.
  - A primary key can be one field – usually a reference of some sort, such as client_ref (see key symbol in Figure 5.6) or a combination of fields, e.g. a hotel room and a date together would uniquely identify a booking record.
- Each field (column) has to be a particular data type.

Linking tables

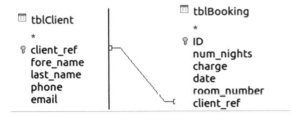

Relational databases are linked together. The primary key of one table can be linked to the **foreign key** of another table. This allows data such as client details to be stored once only. Every time a new booking is made, it can be connected to the one copy of the client details. This avoids data redundancy and reduces the risk of errors.

Data types

When a field is set up, the designer must choose what data type it will be. This makes it easier for the software to validate and process the data. Also, there may be decisions to be made about how much space to allocate to each field.

Data type	Comment	Example of use
Number	Various formats are available in different DBMSs. Some provide separate integer and floating point types.	Number of items ordered (integer) Number of years experience (integer) Temperature (floating point) Distance in km (floating point)
Number (currency)	Allows two digits after a decimal point.	Price Invoice amount
Text	Can often choose how much space to allocate.	Names Telephone numbers (they have leading zeros, plus signs and sometimes spaces) Gender/sex (remember this is not true/false data even though only one of two responses is normally possible)
Date/time	Can use this for dates or times or both. Various formats are possible.	Date of birth Time of appointment Date started employment
Yes/no (Boolean)	Only used for where the data is yes/no or true/false.	Given credit (or not) Entered for exam (or not) Paid (or not)

Forms

These provide a friendly user interface. Data can be input into tables from forms or selected data can be output to the screen in a form. Forms can have objects, such as buttons and drop-down lists, to make them easier to use.

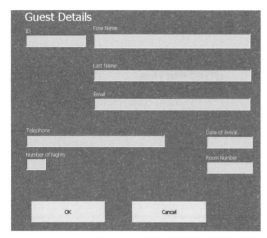

↑ **Figure 5.7 A form with text boxes for data fields and buttons to carry out actions**

Reports

Reports are output from a database. They can be set up to summarise, group and select data.

Room Number	16			
	Date	*Client Ref*	*Number of Nights*	*Name*
	25/09/11	23	1	Pitts
	07/06/11	26	13	Kelly
Room Number	20			
	Date	*Client Ref*	*Number of Nights*	*Name*
	03/02/11	27	14	Sullivan
Room Number	24			
	Date	*Client Ref*	*Number of Nights*	*Name*
	16/08/11	11	10	Barber

↑ **Figure 5.8 A report from a database**

Graphs

Some DBMSs include graphing features so that applications programmers can simply call them up to display data rather than having to write their own display routines.

Queries

A query is used to extract a subset of the data in a database. Queries can combine data from more than one table and present data in whatever order is required. There are two main ways that queries can be created.

Query by example (QBE) uses a graphical interface that lets the user assemble the fields and conditions required for a query.

This query displays the last name and the number of nights stayed by hotel guests but only for those who stayed more than 20 nights.

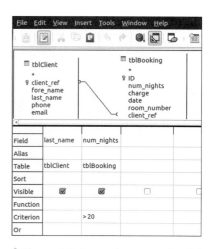

↑ **Figure 5.9 Query by example dialog**

Query language

Alternatively, a query can be built from a query language such as SQL (Structured Query Language). SQL and other query languages make it possible to write programs that extract the data required.

Just as with any programming language, query languages provide operators to check conditions before selecting data to display. The most commonly used comparison operators are AND and OR.

● The AND operator checks that two conditions are true then selects the data that matches these conditions.

● The OR operator checks that either of two conditions is true then selects the data that matches these conditions.

The query in Figure 5.10 checks for clients who match the bookings list AND who stayed longer than 20 nights. This is the same query as before but written in SQL.

```
SELECT "tblClient"."last_name", "tblBooking"."num_nights" FROM "tblBooking", "tblClient" WHERE
"tblBooking"."client_ref" = "tblClient"."client_ref" AND "tblBooking"."num_nights" > 20
```

↑ **Figure 5.10 A query written in SQL**

Here is a query that finds the rooms in the hotel that have a bathroom AND a nice view:

SELECT "room_number", "room_type", "view", "bath"
FROM "tblRoom" WHERE "view" = TRUE AND "bath" = TRUE

Figure 5.11 shows part of the output from the query. Notice that both criteria are true for all rooms.

room_number	room_type	view	bath
5	double	☑	☑
6	double	☑	☑
10	double	☑	☑
16	double	☑	☑
24	twin	☑	☑
30	twin	☑	☑
32	single	☑	☑
35	single	☑	☑
36	single	☑	☑
37	double	☑	☑
40	twin	☑	☑
45	double	☑	☑
46	double	☑	☑

↑ **Figure 5.11 Query output from an AND query**

Figure 5.12 shows the same query with the OR condition. It looks for either a bathroom OR a nice view:

SELECT "room_number", "room_type", "view", "bath"
FROM "tblRoom" WHERE "view" = TRUE OR "bath" = TRUE

This time, the output shows either condition to be true.

Some DBMSs also have their own built-in programming language to help make applications.

room_number	room_type	view	bath
2	twin	☑	☐
3	single	☐	☑
4	twin	☑	☐
5	double	☑	☑
6	double	☑	☑
7	double	☐	☑
8	double	☐	☑
9	double	☑	☐
10	double	☑	☑
11	twin	☑	☐
13	twin	☑	☐
16	double	☑	☑
19	twin	☐	☑

↑ **Figure 5.12 Query output from an OR query**

Modules

A database module is a unit of software that takes care of some particular functionality of a database. Some DBMSs allow you to add such capabilities to a database by writing program code in a language supplied with the DBMS.

Other DBMS features

- Referential integrity: Changes must not be made that are logically impossible. For example, you cannot delete a student if there is a linked record to an exam entry. A DBMS will prevent this.

- Validation: Most DBMSs have simple validation rules available.

- Security features:
  - Groups can be created.
  - Read or write privileges can be assigned to different tables for different groups.

- Automatic backup: Some DBMSs save transactions as they go. This helps prevent data loss. They often have data recovery tools in case of problems occurring.

Check your understanding
Tested

1. Describe four features of a typical DBMS. *(4 marks)*

2. Explain the difference between an entity and a table. *(2 marks)*

3. Describe two ways in which a query can be constructed. *(2 marks)*

4. Give the data that would result from running the following queries on the above database table:

Surname	Forename	Street	City	Sex (m/f)	Years in employment	Salary (£)
Carrillo	Abraham	3792 Etiam St.	Birmingham	m	4	26000
Holland	Sarah	991 Eros Rd.	Colchester	f	6	52000
Hernandez	Blossom	172-934 Ac Street	Birmingham	f	8	87000
Mcleod	Amaya	570-1940 Cras St.	Birmingham	f	4	43089
Vincent	Audra	P.O. Box 342, 6449 Duis Rd.	Birmingham	f	1	78967
Vega	Lucian	P.O. Box 661, 3594 Amet, St.	Worcester	m	3	34566
Cohen	Jessica	P.O. Box 759, 2015 Ante St.	Liverpool	f	4	36755
Gordon	Micah	6419 Gravida Av.	Southampton	m	3	56787

   a) SELECT Surname, City WHERE Sex = "m" *(2 marks)*

   b) SELECT Surname, City WHERE Sex = "m" AND Years in employment > 3 *(2 marks)*

   c) SELECT Surname, Salary WHERE Years in employment < 4 AND Salary > 35000 *(2 marks)*

   d) SELECT Surname WHERE City = "Birmingham" OR Years in employment = 4 *(2 marks)*

5. Construct queries that would produce the following results:

   a) a list of surnames and salaries of all female employees who live in Birmingham *(2 marks)*

   b) a list of surnames, forenames and street address for all employees who have been in employment for 3 years or more or who have salaries greater than £50 000. *(2 marks)*

Go online for answers
Online

Chapter 6 Computer communications and networking

A network is a collection of connected computers plus their peripherals. Each device on a network is called a **node**.

- Computers process and store data.
- The data is represented as binary bit patterns.
- This is a very simple and reliable way to store data.
- Binary data is easy to transmit without errors, because there is only a need to distinguish between 0 and 1.

Most general-purpose computers are networked in order to take advantage of this easy communication. Even if a computer is not part of a local area network, it is likely to be connected to the internet.

LANs

A LAN is a local area network. Most organisations and some individuals have LANs.

A LAN is:

- confined to one site, such as an office or a university campus
- connected using equipment owned by the organisation
- maintained by the organisation (or it may be outsourced).

Networking computers in a LAN has many advantages:

- Central data storage makes data sharing possible and convenient.
- Central data storage makes backups easier to do.
- Computers in a network are easily updated or reconfigured centrally.
- Computer use can easily be monitored.
- Security policies can be centrally administered.
- Users can communicate with each other.
- Expensive peripherals can be shared.

There are few drawbacks to having a LAN but they include:

- Maintenance incurs an expense; specialist staff may be needed.
- Network problems might affect all users.
- Security may be a problem because data is accessible from many places.

WANs

A WAN is a wide area network. It covers a large geographical area which may be a city or even the world. The ultimate WAN is the internet.

- They often connect LANs together.
- They make use of publicly available telecoms facilities.
- They allow a business to function from any location.

> **Exam tip**
> The differences between a LAN and a WAN are regular exam topics.

Network hardware

Special hardware is needed to connect computers. This is to do with creating, receiving and routing electrical signals.

Network interface controllers/cards (NICs)

Each device on a network needs an NIC, also known as a LAN adapter. On most new computers, this is built into the motherboard. They used to be installed as separate cards or circuit boards. Most LANs make use of a network standard called **Ethernet**, so it makes sense to include an adapter as part of a computer because it will work nearly everywhere.

Every NIC has a unique number stored in ROM. This is called its MAC (media access control) address. This allows each node on a network to be identified.

The NIC is a physical device that generates and receives suitable electrical signals. It can also carry out simple addressing by making use of MAC addresses.

Cables

The connections between devices on most LANs are made with copper cable. This is normally a type known as UTP (unshielded twisted pair). This is light and flexible which makes it quite easy to install.

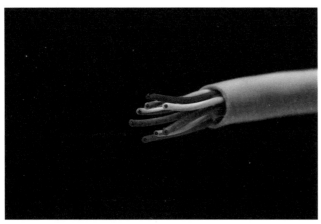

↑ **Figure 6.1 UTP cable**

For longer distances and use outside, fibre-optic cable is often chosen. This transmits signals by using light waves. Fibre-optic cables can carry more signals for their size than copper cables and are cheaper too.

↑ **Figure 6.2 Fibre-optic cable**

Hubs

These are hardware devices that connect many network devices together, making them into a single network segment. (A segment is a defined part of a network.) They have a number of input and output ports which connect to each other. A signal arriving at one is transmitted to all others.

↑ Figure 6.3 A network hub with four ports

Switches

Switches connect network segments or devices. They can also act as **bridges**, which connect more than one network, allowing them to function as one network. A switch differs from a hub by transmitting a message only to the device intended instead of to all connections.

Wireless access points

These allow connection to a LAN without the need for physical cables using standards such as WiFi. Access points are often connected to a **router**. They can save money and effort because new nodes can be added without the need for more cable.

They introduce security risks which have to be dealt with by the use of:

● encryption

● hiding their broadcast identities

● allowing access to only certain MAC addresses.

↑ Figure 6.4 A wireless access point

Routers

A router receives data in the form of packets and forwards them to their destination which is often another router. Routers direct traffic through large networks, notably the internet. Small routers are used in the home to connect individual computers to the Internet Service Provider (ISP).

> **Exam tip**
>
> There are subtle differences between network hardware components. Make sure you have the detail.

1 Describe the purpose of an NIC. *(2 marks)*

2 Distinguish between a network hub and a network switch. *(4 marks)*

3 State three ways in which security can be implemented on a wireless access point. *(3 marks)*

4 Describe the purpose of a router. *(2 marks)*

5 What is a network bridge? *(2 marks)*

Types of network ———————————————————————————————— Revised

There are two principal ways in which networks are organised.

Client–server network

Client–server is by far the most common way to set up a network. One or more **servers** provide services to many **client** machines where the users work.

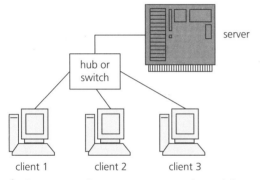

↑ **Figure 6.5 Client–server network model**

Servers are computers that are set up to handle network functions. There may be many on a network. They are typically high-end computers that have enough storage and speed to **serve** the needs of many connected computers. Typical servers include:

● database server, which stores the corporate database

● file server, which stores user files

● mail server, which stores emails received and sent

● print server, which holds and processes print jobs

● web server, which holds a website

● gaming server, which provides online access to games.

Servers do not have to be separate physical machines. It is possible to save hardware expense by having virtual servers, where one physical machine can take on more than one server function.

The advantage of the client–server model is that the network functions are handled by dedicated machines. The clients can provide for the immediate needs of the users. This is an efficient and high speed model.

Peer-to-peer network

In a **peer-to-peer** network, all computers are equal. Each computer serves the needs of the user as well as carrying out networking functions.

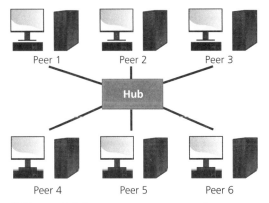

↑ **Figure 6.6 A peer-to-peer network**

Peer-to peer networks are easy to set up but:

● maintenance is more difficult than with a client–server network

● security is poor

● they tend to be slow because of the amount of multitasking.

The peer-to-peer model is useful on the internet where files can be shared directly between users without the need to go through web servers.

Check your understanding ———————————— Tested ☐

1 State three different uses for a network server. *(3 marks)*

2 Explain the difference between a client–server network and a peer-to-peer network. *(4 marks)*

Go online for answers ———————————————————— Online ☐

Network topologies ———————————————————— Revised ☐

Topology refers to the layout of the network components: the cabling and the position of the nodes. There are three principal layouts that you need to know about.

Bus

The computers and other devices are attached to a single backbone. A terminator is attached at each end to prevent reflection of signals. Signals travel in either direction.

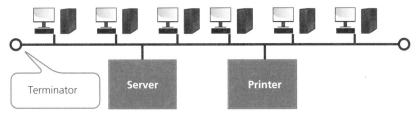

↑ **Figure 6.7 A bus network layout**

Plus points:

● easy to set up

● cheap.

Negative points:

● problems with the backbone can bring the whole network down

● limited distance can be covered

● many data collisions slow the network down.

Star

Client machines are connected to a central switch or hub, which is usually in turn connected to one or more servers. Signals travel in either direction.

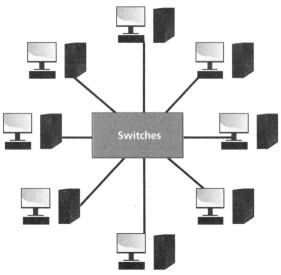

↑ **Figure 6.8 A star network layout**

Plus points:

● robust – problems with a connection do not affect the whole network

● fewer data collisions than bus so faster.

Negative points:

● needs more expertise to maintain

● can be expensive to set up because

● more building work involved

● more network hardware and software needed.

Ring

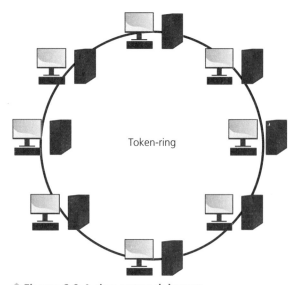

↑ **Figure 6.9 A ring network layout**

Data passes through each node, carried in data units called tokens. Traffic is one-way which prevents collisions.

Plus points:

● very fast – no collisions.

Negative points:

● problems with the backbone can bring the whole network down

● data passes through every node – this makes the network vulnerable to malfunctions.

Exam tip

Network topologies are common in questions although the star configuration is by far the most common in reality.

Check your understanding — Tested

1   Explain why bus networks can often be slow.   *(2 marks)*

2   State two advantages of a star network over a bus network.   *(2 marks)*

Go online for answers — Online

Network technicalities — Revised

Protocols

Sending data in a network requires rules and standards. By sharing these rules, different networks and different devices can talk to each other. A set of rules that covers data communications is called a **protocol**.

Various protocols exist, but the most widely adopted is a set of protocols called **TCP/IP**. This stands for Transmission Control Protocol/Internet Protocol. It encompasses several different protocols. TCP/IP has become the de facto standard for data transmission over the internet.

Hosts are computer systems that are accessed remotely and hold data or other facilities such as web servers. **TCP** is concerned with the connection of hosts. It is not concerned with the nature of the data being sent.

Packets are collections of data forming part of a **message**. A packet is constructed according to rules laid down by the appropriate protocol. A packet contains standard fields such as:

● protocol

● checksum: this is a number that is checked at the receiving end to ensure that the packet has not been corrupted en route

● total length

● sender's address

● receiver's address

● time to live: if it is not delivered, it needs to be destroyed

● packet number: this is used to reconstruct the message in the original order

● data: the part of the message that is being transmitted.

IP is concerned with the construction of the packets.

Packet switching

Packets are sent individually across a network. Packets from a particular message may take different routes according to availability and traffic conditions. They are forwarded from one router to the next. They are assembled to form the complete message at the receiving end. This process is called **packet switching**. It improves the reliability of sending messages because if one route is down or congested, another can be found.

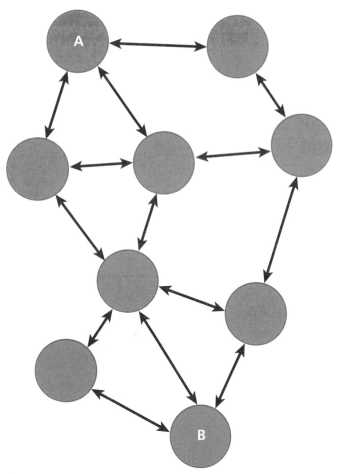

↑ **Figure 6.10 Sending a message from A to B, using many routers**

Other common internet protocols

Protocol	Meaning	Application
DNS	Domain Name System	Translates domain names, such as ocr.org.uk, into IP addresses
TLS/SSL	Transport Layer Security/ Secure Sockets Layer	Cryptographic protocols designed for secure communications
FTP	File Transfer Protocol	For copying files from one host to another
HTTP	Hypertext Transfer Protocol	For distributing hypermedia files – essentially web pages
IMAP	Internet Message Access Protocol	One method for accessing emails
POP3	Post Office Protocol (version 3)	Another method for accessing emails, used by most webmail services
Telnet	–	Allows bi-directional text communications on a network

IP addressing

A letter sent through the mail needs an address in order to be delivered correctly. Similarly, a data packet in a network needs an address for delivery. In TCP/IP networks, including the internet, IP addresses are used. Each computer on a network has an IP address.

An IP address is a 32-bit number such as:
10000011 01101011 00010000 11001000.

Exam tip

Make sure you are able to define the term 'protocol' precisely and quote some examples.

Each group of eight bits is called an octet. Each octet can store numbers ranging from 0 to 255. The address is normally quoted in four groups of decimal numbers, for example 131.107.32.200. IP addresses can be permanently allocated to a device (static addressing), but they can also be allocated as needed (dynamic addressing), so a particular computer will not always have the same IP address.

MAC addressing

MAC means Media Access Control. A MAC address is a unique number stored in each NIC so it can be used to identify a device on a network.

A MAC address is usually given as six pairs of hexadecimal numbers, for example, 01:1F:33:69:BC:14.

Check your understanding   Tested ☐

1   Explain what is meant by a network protocol.   *(3 marks)*
2   Describe two protocols commonly used on the internet.   *(4 marks)*
3   What is a data packet?   *(2 marks)*
4   What is meant by packet switching?   *(3 marks)*
5   What is an IP address?   *(2 marks)*
6   How many different numbers can be represented by an IP address
    octet of eight bits?   *(1 mark)*
7   What is a MAC address?   *(2 marks)*

Go online for answers   Online ☐

Network security   Revised ☐

Networks involve the linking of many devices. This is a potential security threat because data might be accessed from many locations.

Unauthorised access can result in:

- data loss, by deliberate or accidental deletion
- theft of data, which might not even be apparent if it is just copied
- installation of malware
- damage to systems.

Data can also be lost by accident in the case of fires or as a result of malfunctions, war, terrorism or natural hazards.

Backups

To protect against data loss, there needs to be a reliable backup regime. Important data should be copied to a secure facility off site. The cloud is increasingly used for this. The cloud is the provision of online services and storage by third parties.

Backups should be done often enough that the business can continue to function as quickly as possible after a data loss incident and that no data is lost that cannot be recreated.

A partial backup is sometimes enough, where the backup is only of data that has changed since the last backup. The archive flag of a file is set after a backup has been done and it is cleared if the data is changed. This allows automatic partial backups to take place.

Archives

Archived data is old data that is no longer in regular use. It is kept:

● in case future enquiries need it

● for legal reasons.

For example, a school might keep student details after they have left, in case references are required.

Archived data is deleted from the day-to-day system.

Failover

Many systems have a **failover** capacity. This means that software detects a potential disaster or abnormality and immediately transfers operations to a duplicate system. This way, it is hoped that there will be no interruptions to the network services.

Disaster recovery

Organisations need to have a disaster recovery plan. This is a documented plan which covers what to do in the event of catastrophic data loss. It covers:

● prevention

● backups

● who will be involved in recovery

● how to recover the data/systems

● how long it should take.

Network operating systems have features to help make them secure. Typically they are based around authenticating users and assigning them user rights.

Authentication

Users are identified by a user name and verified by a password.

⬆ **Figure 6.11 A login screen**

In many systems, the users are members of groups such as finance or personnel. Permissions can be assigned separately to an individual, a group or anyone else such as a guest user. In each case, permission can be granted to read a file, write to a file (change it) or run it (execute it) if it is a program. In a Unix or Linux system, file permissions can look like this:

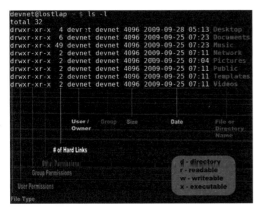

↑ **Figure 6.12 File permissions for eight directories**

The user name says who you are and the operating system can look up your permissions. You then have to **authenticate** who you are with a password. It is important to choose a strong password, that is one that is not easily guessed. Some rules for a strong password are:

● Make it long enough.

● Include numbers and letters.

● Include special characters.

● Change it regularly.

● Don't reveal it to anyone.

● Don't choose something obvious like 'password' or personal information that people might know.

Important data stored on a network is often encrypted. In particular, passwords are stored in an encrypted form so that even if someone gained access to their location, they would still not be decipherable.

Acceptable use policies

Networks, by their nature, are used by many people. Therefore it is important that everything possible is done to make sure that they are kept running and always available. Users normally have to sign up to an acceptable use policy where they undertake to use the facilities responsibly. Typical provisions of an acceptable use policy include:

● not transmitting:

  ● offensive or obscene material

  ● material with the intent to cause annoyance, inconvenience or needless anxiety

  ● material with the intent to defraud

  ● defamatory material

  ● material that infringes the copyright of another person

● not using the network for bulk mailings or marketing

● not accessing unauthorised material

● not wasting staff time

● not corrupting or destroying data

● not violating other users' privacy

● not installing unauthorised software.

> **Exam tip**
>
> You don't need to know these exact details but you should know that security can be very finely tuned.

Check your understanding

1 Identify three ways in which a catastrophic data loss can occur. (3 marks)

2 What needs to be taken into account when deciding on the frequency of taking network backups? (2 marks)

3 What is the difference between a backup and an archive? (3 marks)

4 What does the term 'failover' mean? (2 marks)

5 Describe how a network authenticates a user. (2 marks)

6 State three characteristics of a strong password. (3 marks)

7 State three sensible conditions of an acceptable use policy. (3 marks)

Go online for answers

Online

The internet

The internet is a means of connecting millions of computers and computer networks across the world. The connections are made through routers and servers and a wide variety of transmission media, mostly fibre-optic cables owned by telecoms companies. It is used for the transmission of all sorts of information such as text, graphics, voice, video and computer programs.

No one owns the internet although various organisations contribute to its functioning, such as telecoms businesses and standards organisations.

The **world wide web** is one of the facilities that makes use of the internet. It consists of billions of pages written in HTML or its derivatives.

Most people use the internet to view and use web pages via a web browser, to send emails and to use voice communications.

> **Exam tip**
>
> Make sure you understand that the internet is an infrastructure and that the world wide web is just one of the services that uses it.

Hardware

To connect to the internet, some specialised hardware is needed. The choice of hardware depends on the type of connection that is possible or needed:

● Modem (modulator–demodulator)

Many phone links are analogue. Computers use digital signals. A modem converts between these signals and allows connection to the internet on the POTS (Plain Old Telephone Service) which is still widespread.

● Router

Routers connect networks together. Small routers for home use connect the users' computers to their Internet Service Provider (ISP). These may be combined with a modem or connect to a digital network such as cable TV.

Digital subscriber line (DSL) routers are combined with a modem in order to make use of unused bandwidth in the telephone line which connects with internet links at the telephone exchange (switching centre).

Large corporate users often have routers that connect to a digital line.

Addressing

The internet makes use of IP addressing to identify connected resources.

IP addresses are numbers so they can be hard to remember. The Domain Name System (DNS) is a protocol that connects IP addresses such as 212.58.253.67 to user-friendly names such as bbc.co.uk.

DNS servers maintain databases that match the names against the numbers. When a domain name is entered into a browser, a DNS server is contacted in order to get the correct IP address and then the website required is contacted.

A URL is a Uniform Resource Locator, a standard user-friendly way of describing a resource on the internet. It consists of a domain name and also may include the path to a file and the filename itself.

Internet domain names are made up of standard parts arranged in order. If someone is searching for a good book to help with GCSE computing, the following will come up as a URL:

http://www.hoddereducation.co.uk/Title/9781444177794/OCR_ Computing_for_GCSE_Students_Book.htm

- The domain name is: hoddereducation.co.uk.
- The path on the Hodder server where the information is stored is given by: /Title/9781444177794/.
- The web page with the required information is: OCR_Computing_for_GCSE_Students_Book.htm.

Check your understanding

Tested

1   What is an internet domain name? *(2 marks)*

2   Which two of the following are legal IP addresses?

   a) 121.23.1.45

   b) 256.55.76.8

   c) 1.1.1.1. *(2 marks)*

3   Explain why someone setting up a new internet connection from home would need a router. *(2 marks)*

4   Explain the difference between the internet and the world wide web. *(2 marks)*

5   Explain what a DSL connection is. *(2 marks)*

6   What is the purpose of a modem? *(2 marks)*

Go online for answers

Online

HTML

HTML is Hypertext Markup Language, This is a way of using text files in order to describe a web page. HTML uses tags to instruct a browser how to interpret and display items on a web page.

Here is an example: <h1>A Heading</h1>

<h1> is an opening tag that causes the text to be displayed in large letters.

</h1> is a closing tag that indicates the end of this heading.

The result when processed by a browser is:

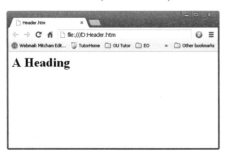

↑ **Figure 6.13 HTML rendered in a browser**

HTML allows the embedding of many elements in a web page such as:

● hyperlinks to other pages or places on the same page

● paragraph markers

● tables

● frames

● images.

HTML also allows the inclusion of code written in scripting languages, such as JavaScript. This can be used to make a web page more dynamic and reactive to the user's actions. For example, data entered in a web form can be validated with some JavaScript code. This code is often implemented client-side. This means that the user's computer runs the code, thereby saving uploading and downloading time.

The inclusion of technologies such as Flash allow web pages to display complex graphics and moving images on sites such as YouTube.

Applets written in languages such as Java can also be embedded in HTML pages.

XML is Extensible Markup Language. This allows the separation of HTML display code and any data that is to be displayed. XML allows users to invent their own tags in order to format data of their own choosing. For example, <PRICE>£4.00</PRICE> can be stored externally to the web page and it will be formatted in whatever way is decided in the HTML code.

Cascading Style Sheets (CSS)

These are files that can be referenced by an HTML page in order to apply a desired style of fonts, colours and other features to a web page. They reduce the complexity of a web page because they are usually stored outside the main HTML text document.

They also reduce the size of the web pages because style elements do not need to be repeated.

CSSs can be used to format pages differently for different platforms such as phones and PCs.

Internet file standards

Revised

Much of the success of the internet is to do with the widespread use of agreed file standards. This allows software and hardware from different sources to interact successfully.

Here are some common examples:

Standard	Meaning	Uses
JPG	Joint Photographic Experts Group	Storing still images, using lossy compression.
GIF	Graphic Interchange Format	Storing bit-mapped images using lossless compression.
PDF	Portable Document Format	Representing documents in the same way no matter what software is being used to display them.
MP3	Moving Picture Experts Group Audio Layer III	Representing digital audio using lossy compression.
MPEG	Moving Picture Experts Group	Representing videos and movie films using lossy compression.

Compression

Files compression means reducing the size of a file. This is usually done in order to:

- save storage space on media, especially on portable devices such as MP3 players
- reduce transmission times on a network, especially the internet.

Compression is particularly important when very large files are being transmitted, such as:

- movie films and videos
- music
- images.

Without compression, movies on DVD and digital TV systems would take up impossibly large amounts of storage and transmission time.

One disadvantage of using compression is that the files have to be decompressed when they are used. This can result in slower operations.

There are two main types of file compression.

- Lossy compression works by removing some of the data from the file. The data that is removed cannot be recovered. Lossy compression is used in file formats such as MP3, JPG and MPEG. Digital photographs can be uploaded to websites in JPG format and different levels of compression can be used. The more an image is compressed, the less detail will be visible.

  Lossy compression algorithms often attempt to remove the least important details such as the higher frequency sounds in a music file that many people cannot hear. Some people think that MP3 sound files are not as good quality as the original CD tracks.

  Lossy compression can produce dramatic savings in file size. Many websites that allow photo sharing will compress photos before displaying them.

- Lossless compression does not store repeated detail, such as lots of blue pixels in a photo that includes the sky. It allows the original file to be reconstructed exactly. A computer program will not work if much of it has been removed to save space.

A 1 MB Image   The same image compressed to 67 KB

↑ Figure 6.14 Lossy compression

Here is one way that lossless compression can be used.

A table of details such as words or pixels is set up. In order to store the data, the table is stored plus an index for each word when it occurs.

1	2	3	4	5	6	7	8	9
If	you	are	not	fired	with	enthusiasm	will	be

So, a sentence could be written from this table such as 1234567289567, thus saving storage space.

Check your understanding   Tested

1. Distinguish between lossy and lossless compression.   *(4 marks)*

2. Explain why images are compressed before being included on a photo-sharing website.   *(3 marks)*

3. Explain the importance of file standards when including external files on a web page.   *(2 marks)*

4. What is HTML?   *(3 marks)*

5. How does XML help to reduce the size of web pages?   *(3 marks)*

Go online for answers   Online

Chapter 7 Programming

Before coding a solution the process needs to be defined.

Algorithms are sets of rules that define a solution to a problem.

Algorithms can be expressed in many ways but typically as a flowchart or in pseudocode.

● A flowchart is a diagrammatic representation of the data flow and structure for the solution.

● Pseudocode is a structured form of English used to define the steps needed to solve a problem.

Flowcharts   Revised ☐

Flowcharts use a standard set of shapes to define different actions:

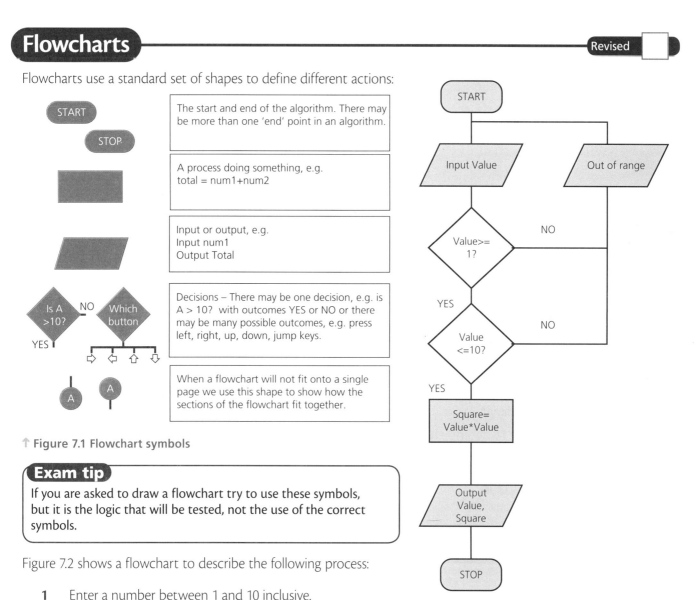

Symbol	Description
START / STOP	The start and end of the algorithm. There may be more than one 'end' point in an algorithm.
(rectangle)	A process doing something, e.g. total = num1+num2
(parallelogram)	Input or output, e.g. Input num1 Output Total
Is A >10? / Which button	Decisions – There may be one decision, e.g. is A > 10? with outcomes YES or NO or there may be many possible outcomes, e.g. press left, right, up, down, jump keys.
(A circles)	When a flowchart will not fit onto a single page we use this shape to show how the sections of the flowchart fit together.

↑ **Figure 7.1 Flowchart symbols**

> **Exam tip**
>
> If you are asked to draw a flowchart try to use these symbols, but it is the logic that will be tested, not the use of the correct symbols.

Figure 7.2 shows a flowchart to describe the following process:

1 Enter a number between 1 and 10 inclusive.

2 Reject values not in range and request the input again.

3 If valid input, calculate the square of the value.

4 Output the value and its square.

↑ **Figure 7.2 A flowchart for a process**

Check your understanding

1 Draw a flowchart to describe the following process:

Input 5 values.

Output their average. *(4 marks)*

2 Draw a flowchart to describe the following process:

Input radius for a circle.

Check it is positive.

Reject and ask for input if not positive.

Output the circumference of the circle if positive. *(4 marks)*

Go online for answers Online

Pseudocode

Revised

Pseudocode is used to describe the program structures and data flows in a structured form of English.

For the flowchart in Figure 7.2, the pseudocode might be:

Repeat

Input a value

Until the value is between 1 and 10

square = value * value

Output value and square

Note we indent the instructions between Repeat and Until to show that this bit is repeated until the condition is met.

> **Exam tip**
>
> Always use indents to show loops and conditions when writing pseudocode.

Check your understanding

Tested

1 Write a pseudocode algorithm to describe how to get the information and output the area of a triangle. *(3 marks)*

2 Write the pseudocode to describe how to calculate the average of 10 numbers. *(6 marks)*

Go online for answers Online

Programming languages

Revised

Machine language

Software has to be provided to the processor in the form of **machine code**:

● This is a stream of binary bit patterns that represent the instructions that are to be carried out.

● The binary bit patterns are **decoded** by the processor's **logic circuits**.

● They are then acted upon or **executed**, one after another.

Machine code is a type of **low-level code**, which means that it works at the level of the computer hardware.

Writing programs in machine code is difficult and time-consuming work:

- Each operation of the processor has to be defined.
- Each machine instruction causes the processor to carry out just one operation.

Nearly all machine code instruction consist of two parts:

- an **opcode**, which tells the processor what to do
- an **operand**, which tells the processor what to do it to.

It is difficult to remember all the bit patterns and what they do.

Assembly language

This is also a **low-level language**.

- As with machine language, each instruction causes just one processor operation.
- Assembly language uses mnemonics to represent instructions.

In machine code, a programmer might write:

000010 00000 00000 00000 10000 000000

Here the first group of bits is the opcode 000010 or 2 in denary. This opcode could mean JUMP, which means the program must continue at the specified address.

The remaining digits are the operand. This is the address 00000 00000 00000 10000 000000 or 1024 in denary.

With assembly language, the programmer doesn't have to remember all these bits.

To jump to address 1024, the programmer might write JMP 1024.

Software called an assembler translates the mnemonic JMP 1024 into the machine code bit pattern that the processor needs.

Exam tip

You do not need to learn any assembly language commands, just the principles.

High-level languages

High-level languages do not have the same one-to-one correspondence between commands and machine code instructions as assembler.

A high-level language command may represent several machine code instructions:

- In a high-level language we can usually multiply two numbers together in one command.
- At machine level this is not possible and it has to be done by repeated addition.

High-level commands have to be turned into the binary instructions the machine can understand; this process is called translation.

There are two basic ways of translating high-level code to machine code:

- Compiler: converts the whole code into machine code before running it
- Interpreter: converts the code one instruction at a time, running each instruction before translating the next.

Source code is the code written by the programmer.

A compiler translates this source code into an object code in machine language. Object code runs independently of the source code and translator.

An interpreter does not create object code and the source code must be translated each time it is run. This means interpreted languages need the source code and translator present every time the code is run.

> **Exam tip**
>
> You should be able to state these advantages and disadvantages when asked to compare translators.

Translator	Advantages	Disadvantages
Assembler	Precise and direct instructions to the computer hardware	Difficult to code Limited range of commands available
Compiler	Compiler not needed on target machine Code runs quickly once compiled Difficult for others to modify without access to the source code	Initial compilation can be slow Errors are generated for all the code at once, making it difficult to debug
Interpreter	Executes one statement at a time so easy to debug Code can be developed and tested in stages Can be more portable since the code will run on any machine with an interpreter available	Interpreter needed on target machine The interpreter takes up space in memory Code executes more slowly Easy to modify since source code is provided

Check your understanding — Tested

1 What are the main advantages of a high-level language over a low-level language? *(4 marks)*

2 Compare an interpreter and a compiler for use by a student learning to program. *(4 marks)*

3 What are the advantages of compiling code for commercial distribution? *(4 marks)*

Go online for answers — Online

Integrated development environment — Revised

Translators usually include an Integrated Development Environment (IDE) to help programmers.

Typical features in an IDE are:

- source code editor – a text editing area organises the code including indenting structures and colour coding command words, variables and comments
- error diagnostics and debugger – warnings identify potential problems with the code and listing errors found in the code
- run-time environment – allows the developer to run the code during development to check for logical errors
- translator (compiler or interpreter) – compiles or interprets the source code into runnable machine code
- automation tools:
  - Wizards autocomplete code as it is typed.
  - Auto documentation to track variables, sub-routines and comments as the project is developed. (This produces a text file that can be used for maintenance of the program.)

This is the IDE from Visual Studio 10 for editing forms.

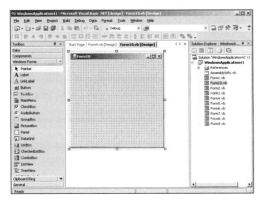

↑ **Figure 7.3 Visual Studio IDE**

Exam tip

You should be able to identify and say how each of these IDE features helps the developer create a program more effectively.

Check your understanding

1 What are the main features of an IDE?   *(4 marks)*

2 How do the features of an IDE help to create maintainable code?   *(4 marks)*

Tested

Go online for answers

Online

Control flow in imperative languages

Revised

Sequence

The path through the program follows a list of instructions, carried out in order.

For example, a program to input two numbers then output their total:

Input num1

Input num2

total = num1 + num2

Output total

Selection

The path through the program is decided by looking at a condition then following one of a set of paths based on the result of that condition.

For example the IF–THEN–ELSE construct allows the program to take one of several paths based on the outcome of a comparison.

To determine if a person can go onto a ride in a theme park we might use:

Get height

IF height >= 1.5m THEN

    Allow onto ride

ELSE

    Do not allow onto ride

ENDIF

More complex cases, for example a quiz, may use a CASE statement or the ELSE IF statement:

> Get answer
>
> IF answer = "Paris" THEN
>
> > Output "Sorry incorrect, that is the capital of France"
>
> ELSE IF answer = "Barcelona"
>
> > Output "Sorry right country but not the capital"
>
> ELSE IF answer = "S"
>
> > Output "Funny, but no"
>
> ELSE IF answer = "Madrid"
>
> > Output "Well done"
>
> ELSE IF answer <> "Madrid"
>
> > Output "Incorrect the answer was Madrid"

Using a case statement:

> Get answer
>
> Select Case answer of

Paris:	Output "Sorry incorrect, that is the capital of France"
Barcelona:	Output "Sorry right country but not the capital"
S:	Output "Funny, but no"
Madrid:	Output "Well done"
Otherwise	Output "Incorrect the answer was Madrid"

Iteration

The program completes a set of instructions several times until a condition is met.

To make a program execute a set of commands several times we can use a **count-controlled loop** or a **condition-controlled loop**.

In a **count-controlled loop** we use an index value to tell the program how many times to complete the loop. For example, to print a 'times table':

```
FOR k = 1 TO 12
    OUTPUT k "times 7 is" k*7
NEXT k
```

We can tell the loop to use different steps, for example to count backwards:

> For k = 10 to 1 step −1

Or to go up in steps of 2:

> For k = 0 to 12 step 2

It is possible to set up a loop that would never finish, for example:

> For k = 1 to 10 step −2,

but these are usually identified by the programming language as an error.

In a **condition-controlled loop** we tell the program to either stop executing the commands when a condition is reached or tell it to execute the commands while a condition is true.

- **Repeat–Until** executes the code that follows until a condition is true.

- **While–Endwhile** executes the code that follows while a condition is true.

For example, a program to collect numbers from a user until they decide they have entered all the data, and output the total value and the average of the values.

```
count = 0
total = 0
REPEAT
    INPUT "enter number" value
    count = count + 1
    total = total + value
    INPUT "more numbers ?" more
UNTIL more <> "yes"
OUTPUT total, total/count
```

```
count = 0
total = 0
more = "yes"
WHILE more = "yes"
    INPUT "enter number" value
    count = count + 1
    total = total + value
    INPUT "more numbers ?" more
ENDWHILE
OUTPUT total, total/count
```

Check your understanding
Tested

1 Identify which control flow the following programs will use:

   a) Deciding whether to give a discount to a customer for having a loyalty card.

   b) Inputting 10 numbers to be totalled.

   c) Setting up the computer when it is switched on. *(3 marks)*

2 Write the pseudocode using a Repeat–Until loop to output the first five square numbers. *(2 marks)*

3 Do this again using a While–Endwhile loop. *(3 marks)*

Go online for answers
Online

Data types
Revised

Data type	Description	Example of use	Space required
Integer	Whole number values, positive or negative with no decimal or fractional part	Used to store data such as quantities	Typically 2 or 4 bytes
Real	Numbers with a decimal or fractional part	Used to store values such as price, weight or height	Typically 4 or 8 bytes
Character	Single alphanumeric character	Used to store a single character such as a letter, digit or symbol such as A, h, 6 or &	1 byte
String	Any string of alphanumeric characters	Used to store descriptions, telephone numbers or any data that will not be used in arithmetic calculations	1 byte per character in the string
Boolean	One of two values: TRUE or FALSE	Used to store flags or the results of decisions	1 bit (but usually 1 byte is allocated)

Check your understanding — Tested

An online retailer keeps data about stock in their database. Items of stock are identified by a single letter, F for furniture, G for garden, P for pet, followed by a four-digit number. They also store the quantity in stock, the retail price and whether there are more on order or not.

Complete the information in this table: *(12 marks)*

Variable name	Typical value	Data type	Typical size
ItemCode			
QuantityInStock			
RetailPrice			
OnOrder			

Go online for answers — Online

Variables and constants — Revised

A **variable** or **constant** is a named storage space reserved in memory to store the value associated with that variable name or constant.

Variables and constants are often **declared** at the start of a program to avoid the danger of any data already stored in that location by a previous program being used and giving false results.

Variables and constants should be given **meaningful names** in order to make it clear what they represent and to make the code easier to follow.

Check your understanding — Tested

1 Constant VAT = 0.2

  Input Wholesale Price

  Retail Price = Wholesale Price + Wholesale Price * VAT

  Output Retail Price

  In the code above:

  a) Identify a constant. *(1 mark)*

  b) Identify the variables. *(1 mark)*

2 Describe the difference between a variable and a constant. *(2 marks)*

3 What is a variable? *(2 marks)*

4 What data type will be used for Retail Price and why? *(2 marks)*

Go online for answers — Online

Operations

There are several **standard mathematical operations** that a computer can perform. The results are usually **assigned** to a variable.

The **assignment operator** may be **=** or may be **==** or **:=** or **::=**, but these all mean the same thing: the result from the right-hand side is to be stored in the variable on the left-hand side.

Operator	Name	Example	Comment
+	Add	value := num1 + num2	Adds num1 and num2 and stores the result in value. If num1 = 3 and num2 = 4, value = 7
−	Subtract	value := num1 − num2	Subtracts num2 from num1 and stores the result in value. If num1 − 7 and num2 = 2, value = 5
*	Multiply	value := num1 * num2	Multiplies num1 by num2 and stores the result in value. If num1 = 7 and num2 = 2, value = 14
/	Divide	value := num1/num2	Divides num1 by num2 and stores the result in value. If num1 = 12 and num2 = 3, value = 4
MOD	Modulus	value := num1 MOD num2	Returns the remainder (modulus) when num1 is divided by num2 and stores this in value. If num1 = 23 and num2 = 5, value = 3
DIV	Quotient	value := num1 DIV num2	Returns the whole number part (quotient) when num1 is divided by num2 and stores this in value. If num1 = 23 and num2 = 5, value = 4

Check your understanding

What value is stored in the variable Result if

a) Result = 7/2   *(1 mark)*

b) Result = 27 MOD 4   *(1 mark)*

c) Result = 36 MOD 6   *(1 mark)*

d) Result = 23 DIV 4   *(1 mark)*

e) Result = 36 DIV 6?   *(1 mark)*

Go online for answers

Comparison operators

Comparison operators are used to compare two values.

Comparison operator	Meaning
=	Is equal to
>	Is greater than
<	Is less than
<>	Is not equal to
>=	Is greater than or equal to
<=	Is less than or equal to

TRUE or **FALSE** are returned depending on the values being compared. For example the comparison 5 < 7 will return TRUE, but 7 < 5 will return FALSE.

Comparisons are also frequently used with AND, OR and NOT logic operators:

● The comparison 5 < 7 OR 7 < 5 will return TRUE because one of the comparisons is true.

● The comparison 5 < 7 AND 7 < 5 will return FALSE because AND requires both values to be TRUE.

The statement IF age >= 12 AND height >= 1.5 will return the following results for the given values:

age	height	age >= 12	height >= 1.5	Result
11	1.6	FALSE	TRUE	FALSE
14	1.48	TRUE	FALSE	FALSE
12	1.5	TRUE	TRUE	TRUE

Exam tip

Be careful about the use of = as an assignment as in **x = 5 + 4** where **x = 9** and as a comparison as in **IF 5 = 4**, where the comparison returns FALSE.

Check your understanding

What is the result returned by the following conditions:

a) num1 > num2 if num1 = 7 and num2 = 5 *(1 mark)*

b) num1 <= num2 if num1 = 7 and num2 = 5 *(1 mark)*

c) num1 <> num2 if num1 = 7 and num2 = 5 *(1 mark)*

d) num1 <> num2 AND num1 < num2 if num1 = 7 and num2 = 5 *(1 mark)*

e) num1 <> num2 OR num1 = num2 if num1 = 7 and num2 = 5? *(1 mark)*

Go online for answers

Tested

Online

Operator priority

Revised

The order in which operators are applied can be important. The priority for operations is:

1 Operations inside brackets are dealt with first

2 Unary operators such as the minus sign and NOT

3 Multiplication and division: *, /, MOD, DIV

4 Addition and subtraction: +, −

5 Boolean operators, such as AND and OR.

5*(7−3) means 5*4 = 20

5*7−3 means 35−3 = 32

What value is assigned to the variable value if:

a) value = 17−3*4   *(1 mark)*

b) value = (17−3)*4   *(1 mark)*

c) value = 7*8/2   *(1 mark)*

d) value = 7+8/4   *(1 mark)*

e) value = 17 MOD 3+4   *(1 mark)*

f) value = 17 MOD (3+4)   *(1 mark)*

Go online for answers ──────────────────────────────────── Online

Arrays ── Revised

Variables should be given meaningful names to make it clear what they represent. If we need a number of variables all with the same name then we can use an array. An **array** is a set of variables with the same name (or **identifier**) and an **index** number to identify the different variables.

For example, a set of names for 20 people could be stored in the array names using name(1), name(2), name(3), etc up to name(20).

If we have the following data stored in the array names:

1	2	3	4	5	6	7	8	9	...
Harry	Jayne	Ranjit	Sophie	Duncan	Millie	Chi	...	...	...

then name(4) is Sophie and name(5) is Duncan.

If we assign the value Aamir to the variable name(8) then the data will be updated to:

1	2	3	4	5	6	7	8	9	...
Harry	Jayne	Ranjit	Sophie	Duncan	Millie	Chi	Aamir	...	...

> **Exam tip**
>
> Many languages number arrays from 0, so declaring an array called items with 10 values will often give a set of variables items(0) to items(9).

Testing ── Revised

Good program design and the use of an **Integrated Development Environment (IDE)** will eliminate many errors from a program.

Syntax errors are errors in the use of the language rules and these are often identified by the IDE.

Examples of syntax errors include:

● variables not being declared before use

● assignment being used incorrectly, e.g. **3 + 4 = x** is incorrect and it should be **x = 3 + 4**

● variable names incorrect, e.g. spelling not the same as the declared variable.

If syntax errors are identified and eliminated then the program may still not perform as expected due to logic errors.

Logic errors may be generated by variables not taking the values expected or decisions that do not allow the program to complete. Causes of logic errors include:

● conditions that cannot be met in conditional statements

● infinite loops (looping so that the condition is never met)

● incorrect algorithms (the algorithm does not do what it is meant to)

● incorrect expressions (calculations that are incorrect or have missing brackets).

This can lead to run-time errors such as:

● division by zero

● programs that do not complete

● the memory is filled with data and we get stack overflow messages

● incorrect output.

Good programming practice

The use of meaningful variable names and structured code make testing and future maintenance of the code more effective.

Checking data at the input stage for validity minimises run-time errors.

Test data covering many potential situations will eliminate many potential errors.

Test data should be chosen to cover valid, invalid, extreme and erroneous situations and the expected outcomes should be identified.

For example to test an input value is in range when only the whole number values 1, 2, 3, 4 or 5 are acceptable:

> **Exam tip**
>
> Questions will not expect full test plans but you should think about using a range of test types in your answers.

Test	Data	Reason	Expected result
Valid	3	In range 1 to 5 and whole number	Accepted
Valid extreme value in range	5	In range but at extreme end of range	Accepted
Invalid	2.3	Not a whole number	Rejected
Invalid	R	Not a number	Rejected
Invalid	6	Whole number but outside range	Rejected

1 What is meant by 'syntax error'? Give an example of a syntax error. *(2 marks)*

2 What is meant by 'run-time error'? Give an example of a run-time error. *(2 marks)*

3 A = 3

   B = 5

   A + B = C

   The above code contains an error. What is the error and what type of error is it? *(2 marks)*

4 INPUT customer

   INPUT cash

   IF customer = 'yes' AND cash > 50 THEN

         rate =11

   ELSE IF customer = 'no' AND cash < 50 THEN

         rate = 9

      ELSE

         rate = 10

      ENDIF

   ENDIF

   OUTPUT cash*rate

   For the algorithm above, state what the output will be for the following input values:

   a) customer = no, cash = 20 *(1 mark)*

   b) customer = yes, cash = 100 *(1 mark)*

   c) customer = yes, cash = 20 *(1 mark)*

   d) customer = no, cash = 60. *(1 mark)*

Go online for answers ──────────────────────── Online

My notes

My notes

My notes

My notes

My notes